THE LANGUAGE GYM
SPEAKING BOOKLET I

Edited by Jérôme Nogues & Aurélie Lethuilier

FRENCH
SENTENCE BUILDERS
TRILOGY
PART 1
A lexicogrammar approach

SPEAKING BOOKLET

About the authors

Gianfranco Conti taught for 25 years at schools in Italy, the UK and in Kuala Lumpur, Malaysia. He has also been a university lecturer, holds a Master's degree in Applied Linguistics and a PhD in metacognitive strategies as applied to second language writing. He is now an author, a popular independent educational consultant and professional development provider. He has written around 2,000 resources for the TES website, which have awarded him the Best Resources Contributor in 2015. He has co-authored the best-selling and influential book for world languages teachers, "The Language Teacher Toolkit" and "Breaking the sound barrier: Teaching learners how to listen", in which he puts forth his Listening As Modelling methodology. Gianfranco writes an influential blog on second language acquisition called The Language Gym, co-founded the interactive website language-gym.com and the Facebook professional group Global Innovative Language Teachers (GILT). Last but not least, Gianfranco has created the instructional approach known as E.P.I. (Extensive Processing Instruction).

Dylan Viñales has taught for 15 years, in schools in Bath, Beijing and Kuala Lumpur in state, independent and international settings. He lives in Kuala Lumpur. He is fluent in five languages, and gets by in several more. Dylan is, besides a teacher, a professional development provider, specialising in E.P.I., metacognition, teaching languages through music (especially ukulele) and cognitive science. In the last five years, together with Dr Conti, he has driven the implementation of E.P.I. in one of the top international schools in the world: Garden International School. This has allowed him to test, on a daily basis, the sequences and activities included in this book with excellent results (his students have won language competitions both locally and internationally). He has designed an original Spanish curriculum, bespoke instructional materials, based on Reading and Listening as Modelling (RAM and LAM). Dylan co-founded the fastest growing professional development group for modern languages teachers on Facebook, Global Innovative Languages Teachers, which includes over 12,000 teachers from all corners of the globe. He authors an influential blog on modern language pedagogy in which he supports the teaching of languages through E.P.I. Dylan is the lead author of Spanish content on the Language Gym website and oversees the technological development of the site

Ronan Jézéquel has taught for 15 years, in schools in Frimley, Brighton and Kuala Lumpur in state and international settings. He lives in Sabah, Malaysia. He is fluent in three languages, and gets by in several more. Ronan is, besides a teacher, a keen mountain biker and an outdoor enthusiast. In the last five years, together with Dr Conti and Dylan Viñales, he has contributed to the implementation of E.P.I. in one of the top international schools in the world: Garden International School. This has allowed him to test, on a daily basis, the sequences and activities included in this book with excellent results. Ronan is the lead author of French content on The Language Gym website and he also brings the competitive element from his sporty background to TLG with the design of live games and features such as our leaderboard.

Acknowledgements

We would like to thank our editor, Jérôme Nogues, for his tireless work, proofreading, editing and advising on this book. He is a talented, accomplished professional who work at the highest possible level and add value at every stage of the process. Not only this, but they are also lovely, good-humoured colleagues who go above and beyond, and make the hours of collaborating a real pleasure.

Thanks to Flaticon.com for providing access to a limitless library of engaging icons, clipart and images, which we have used to make this book more user-friendly and engaging for students.

Additionally, our gratitude to the MFL Twitterati for their ongoing support of E.P.I. and the Sentence Builders book series.

In particular a shoutout to our team of incredible educators who helped in checking all the units of this volume: Aurélie Lethuilier, Jérôme Nogues, Lorène Martine Carver, Ester Borin, Christian Moretti, Ryan Cockrell, Anna Vila, Sonja Fedrizzi, Sarah Castillejo & Inés Głowacka. It is thanks to your time, patience, professionalism and detailed feedback that we have been able to produce such a refined and highly accurate product.

Merci à tous,
Gianfranco & Dylan

Dedication

For Catrina
-Gianfranco

For Ariella & Leonard
-Dylan

For Mariana
-Ronan

Introduction

Hello and welcome to the first Speaking Skills book designed to be an accompaniment to our French, Extensive Processing Instruction course.

How to use this book

This book has been designed as a resource to use in conjunction with the E.P.I. approach and teaching strategies in a bid to scaffold oral communication by gradually moving from highly structured tasks (e.g. 'Oral Ping Pong', 'No snakes no ladders', 'Communicative drills') to semi-structured ones (e.g. 'Surveys', 'Things in Common', 'Detectives and Informants').

The activities in this book should be carried out after an intensive listening and reading phase, in which the students have been flooded with highly comprehensible input containing the target vocabulary and grammar structures, thereby processing them receptively many times over.

If following the MARS EARS framework, teachers may want to stage two or three 'chunking-aloud' games, such as 'Mind reading', 'Sentence stealer', 'Lie detector', etc. in order to warm the students up, consolidate good pronunciation and refine their decoding skills.

Also, prior to playing oral retrieval practice games such as 'Oral Ping-Pong', it is recommended that the students do some retrieval practice in writing. This can be done through digital tools, worksheets, mini whiteboards and may be teacher and/or student led.

Finally, it is recommended that before carrying out the fluency-building games 'Faster', 'Fast and Furious', 'Fluency cards' and Trapdoor', the students be given a few minutes to plan the tasks individually or with peers in order to decrease the potential for cognitive overload and subsequent errors that speaking at increasing speed rate may elicit due to the challenging nature of the task.

What's inside

The book contains 15 units which concern themselves with specific communicative functions, such as 'Describing people's appearance and personality', 'Saying what you like and dislike' or 'Saying what you and others do in your free time'.

Each unit includes a sentence builder with the target constructions and vocabulary followed by a series of tried and tested Conti E.P.I. speaking games sequenced so as to pose a gradually increasing degree of challenge. The speaking games included are:

o Oral Ping Pong	o Communicative Drills
o Find Someone Who	o Fluency Cards
o No Snakes No Ladders	o Trapdoor
o Staircase Translation	o Things in Common
o Faster!	o Detectives & Informants
o Fast & Furious	o Information Gap Tasks

As already noted, the above games are sequenced in ascending order of linguistic and cognitive challenge. The focus is on gradually building up students' fluency and autonomous competence. These games fall in the 'Structured Production', 'Routinization' and 'Spontaneity' phases in Dr Conti's **MARS EARS** pedagogical cycle, which is central to his E.P.I. approach.

Many thanks for reading this. We hope that both you and your students will find this book useful and enjoyable.

Gianfranco and Dylan

SENTENCE BUILDERS TRILOGY - PART 1 SPEAKING BOOKLET

TABLE OF CONTENTS

How to play the games – INSTRUCTIONS

ORAL PING PONG

Students work with a partner.

1. Student A starts by reading out his/her first sentence **in English**. Student B must translate into French.

2. Student A checks the answer on their sheet. If correct, Student B gets 3 points (100% accurate), 2 points (1 error), or 1 point (verb correct).

3. Student B then reads out his/her first sentence **in English**, Student A translates, and B checks and so on. It is called 'Oral ping-pong translation' because students are firing phrases at each other to translate and score points. **The person with the most points after 10 mins wins.**

NOTE: As a follow-up, students should **write** the translations in the gaps provided.

FIND SOMEONE WHO

1. Students are given a card each and a grid to fill in (both provided in each unit of this book).

2. Students must take turns asking the key questions (provided) and then listening to the information provided by fellow students on their cards.

3. If a student finds someone who matches the criteria in the grid, they write down the person's name.

TIP: you will need to set high expectations and then monitor students to make sure they engage in target language and use their speaking & listening skills. Some students may try and bend the rules by copying from friends.

NO SNAKES NO LADDERS

Students work in triads. You will need one dice per table and a copy of both the English & French board.

1. One student is the referee and two students are the players.

2. The referee has access to the translations (via a copy of either the English or the French board).

3. Students role a dice and then move their counter forward. They must then translate the language in the box where their counter falls.

4. If a student translates correctly, as confirmed by the referee, they can roll again.

5. If a student cannot translate the content of a square, the referee must tell them the answer, and it is then the other player's turn.

6. When a student wins the game, the referee changes, in order to allow students to alternate roles.

TIP: We recommend starting from Target Language to English, and then after a couple of rounds, or whenever students are ready, then working from English to Target Language.

STAIRCASE TRANSLATION

Students work with a partner.

1. Students must **translate aloud** the paragraph as quickly as possible.

2. Once the whole paragraph has been successfully translated aloud, students write down the translation into the box.

FASTER

Students alternate the role of player and referee.

1. Students translate aloud a number of sentences in front of a referee.

2. The student referee gives a time and feedback on accuracy.

3. The student listens to feedback and then repeats the process with a second, third, fourth, referee with an aim to improving in terms of speed and accuracy on each attempt.

 TIP: Make sure that referees have a visible timer, to increase motivation!

FAST & FURIOUS

Similar to FASTER, but students work from gapped target language sentences.

COMMUNICATIVE DRILLS
Students alternate the role of player and referee.
1. Students work with a partner to translate short dialogues from English to French.
2. The student referee monitors the game and provides help and feedback on accuracy.
3. Once the students have correctly translated all the boxes out loud, the game is over.
TIPS:
- We recommend a rule that whenever the game ends, the referee then faces the winner, or the loser.
- This game can be played with both players working together to translate the squares (collaborating and helping each other), or as a timed challenge (if students are more confident) to translate all 6/9 squares individually with the fastest time.

FLUENCY CARDS
Students alternate the role of player and referee.
Played like FASTER, students create sentences in Target Language to match the content of the stimulus grid. There is a mixture of text and pictures in order to help create more varied & multi-modal connections to the lexical items and structures being studied.

THINGS IN COMMON
This activity works like the final SURVEY activity, but focuses on asking closed questions, such as "do you prefer *football* or *basketball?*"
1. Students are given some time to think about their own answers to the questions.
2. Students then ask their peers the questions and make a note of any students that have matching answers (therefore 'things in common')
TIPS: Students can be given a set time to speak to as many of their peers as possible, or a race to find a certain number of people with a certain number of things in common.

TRAPDOOR
Students alternate the role of player and referee. Played like FASTER, students translate a set of sentences using the information in the table, which is chunked into several columns, as a support.

DETECTIVES & INFORMANTS
This is a collaborative class game, along the lines of **Find Someone Who**.
1. Divide the class into 2 halves.
2. One half - **the detectives**, have a grid with missing information that they need to fill in. They have one grid per team that needs filling in. This grid must stay at a central location (such as a team home base).
3. One half – **the informants** have pieces of paper with answers to questions.
4. The detectives must ask questions to the informants and then return to their home base to help their team fill in the grid.

INFORMATION GAP TASK
Without viewing the other person's table, the two students need to complete the table asking each other questions in French in order to fill in the gaps.
1. Students take turns to ask each other questions and fill in the answers.
2. The game ends when both tables are fully filled in.

SURVEY
Students ask each other the key questions that have been practised throughout the unit. They then note down key information, either in English or in French on their grid. As a follow-up you could ask students to write a summary of a friend's information, either in 1st or 3rd person.

Comment tu t'appelles? *What is your name?*	**Je m'appelle** *My name is*	Charles Marie
Comment ça va aujourd'hui? *How are you today?*	**Ça va bien, merci** *I am well, thanks*	
Comment vas-tu? *How are you?*	**Je vais assez bien. Et toi?** *I am quite well. And you?*	

					MASC	FEM
Bonjour *Hello* **Bonsoir** *Good evening* **Salut** *Hi* **Au revoir** *Goodbye* **Bonne nuit** *Good night* **De rien** *You're welcome* **Merci** *Thank you* **Enchanté(e)** *Nice to meet you* **D'accord** *OK*	**aujourd'hui ça va** *today I am* **je vais** *I am*	**très bien** *very well* **bien** *well* **comme-ci, comme-ça** *(feeling)* *so-so* **mal** *(feeling)* *bad* **très mal** *(feeling)* *very bad*	**mais je suis** *but I am (feeling)* **car je suis** *because I am (feeling)*	**assez** *quite* **très** *very* **un peu** *a bit*	**détendu** *relaxed* **en colère** *angry* **énervé** *annoyed* **fatigué** *tired* **heureux** *happy* **malade** *sick* **stressé** *stressed* **triste** *sad*	**détendue** **en colère** **énervée** **fatiguée** **heureuse** **malade** **stressée** **triste**

UNIT 0 – FIND SOMEONE WHO – Student Cards

Je m'appelle Marc. Aujourd'hui, je suis malade. **MARC**	Je m'appelle Jules. Aujourd'hui, je vais très mal. **JULES**	Je m'appelle Marine. Aujourd'hui, je suis stressée. **MARINE**	Je m'appelle Louis. Aujourd'hui, je suis malade. **LOUIS**
Je m'appelle Léa. Aujourd'hui, je suis énervée. **LÉA**	Je m'appelle Suzanne. Aujourd'hui, je suis heureuse. **SUZANNE**	Je m'appelle Anne. Aujourd'hui, je suis très détendue. **ANNE**	Je m'appelle Patricia. Aujourd'hui, je suis énervée. **PATRICIA**
Je m'appelle Rose. Aujourd'hui, je suis très triste. **ROSE**	Je m'appelle Marie-Hélène. Aujourd'hui, je suis très fatiguée. **MARIE-HÉLÈNE**	Je m'appelle Pierre. Aujourd'hui, je vais très mal. **PIERRE**	Je m'appelle Martine. Aujourd'hui, je suis heureuse. **MARTINE**
Je m'appelle Denis. Aujourd'hui, je suis en colère. **DENIS**	Je m'appelle Charles. Aujourd'hui, je vais très bien. **CHARLES**	Je m'appelle Paul. Aujourd'hui, je vais bien. **PAUL**	Je m'appelle David. Aujourd'hui, je ne suis pas triste. **DAVID**

UNIT 0 – FIND SOMEONE WHO – Student Grid

	Find someone who...	Name
1.	...is ill today.	
2.	...is annoyed.	
3.	...is very tired.	
4.	...is feeling angry.	
5.	...is feeling very relaxed.	
6.	...is feeling stressed.	
7.	...is feeling well.	
8.	...is feeling happy.	
9.	...is feeling very sad.	
10.	...is feeling very bad.	
11.	...is feeling very well.	
12.	...is not sad today	

UNIT 0 – ORAL PING PONG – Person A

ENGLISH 1	FRENCH 1
I am very well today.	Aujourd'hui, je vais très bien.
I am tired.	
I am annoyed today.	Aujourd'hui, je suis énervé(e).
I am stressed.	
I am relaxed today.	Aujourd'hui, je suis détendu(e).
I am feeling bad.	
I am feeling so-so today.	Aujourd'hui, je vais comme-ci, comme-ça.
I am happy.	
I am sad today.	Aujourd'hui, je suis triste.
I am angry.	

UNIT 0 – ORAL PING PONG – Person B

ENGLISH	FRENCH
I am very well today.	
I am tired.	Je suis fatigué(e).
I am annoyed today.	
I am stressed.	Je suis stressé(e).
I am relaxed today.	
I am feeling bad.	Je vais mal.
I am feeling so-so today.	
I am happy.	Je suis heureux/heureuse.
I am sad today.	
I am angry.	Je suis en colère.

No Snakes No Ladders

START	1 Hello.	2 Good evening.	3 What is your name?	4 My name is Pierre.	5 How are you?	6 I am tired (M).	7 I am annoyed.
15 I am feeling bad.	14 I am very well.	13 I am very angry.	12 I am very relaxed.	11 I am stressed.	10 I am tired.	9 My name is Andréa.	8 What is your name?
16 How are you?	17 I am happy (M).	18 I am sad.	19 I am very happy (F).	20 I am very sad.	21 I am feeling very bad.	22 I am stressed.	23 I am very annoyed.
FINISH	30 Good night.	29 I am so-so.	28 I am very happy (M).	27 I am quite relaxed.	26 How are you?	25 I am feeling well.	24 I am tired.

No Snakes No Ladders

DÉPART	1 Bonjour.	2 Bonsoir.	3 Comment tu t'appelles?	4 Je m'appelle Pierre.	5 Comment ça va?	6 Je suis fatigué.	7 Je suis énervé(e).
15 Je vais mal.	14 Je vais très bien.	13 Je suis très en colère.	12 Je suis très détendu(e).	11 Je suis stressé(e).	10 Je suis fatigué(e).	9 Je m'appelle Andréa.	8 Comment tu t'appelles?
16 Comment ça va?	17 Je suis heureux.	18 Je suis triste.	19 Je suis très heureuse.	20 Je suis très triste.	21 Je vais très mal.	22 Je suis stressé(e).	23 Je suis très énervé(e).
ARRIVÉE	30 Bonne nuit.	29 Je vais comme-ci, comme-ça.	28 Je suis très heureux.	27 Je suis assez détendu(e).	26 Comment ça va?	25 Je vais bien.	24 Je suis fatigué(e).

UNIT 0 – STAIRCASE TRANSLATION

Hello.

Hello. My name is Pierre.

Hello. My name is Pierre. Today I am very well.

Hello. My name is Pierre. Today I am very well because I am happy.

Hello. My name is Pierre. Today I am very well because I am happy and relaxed.

* Hello. My name is Pierre. Today I am very well because I am happy and relaxed. How are you?

* Translate the
last step here:

⏱ UNIT 0 – FASTER! 🚀

Say:
1. Hello.
2. How are you?
3. I am very well. And you?
4. Thank you.
5. I am happy and relaxed.
6. Today I am feeling very tired.
7. What is your name?
8. My name is Philippe.
9. Today I am angry.
10. Good night.

	Time	Mistakes	Referee's name
1			
2			
3			
4			

UNIT 0 – FAST & FURIOUS – Version 1

1. Salut, je _______ très bien, mais je suis un _______ fatigué.

Hi, I am feeling very well, but I am a bit tired.

2. _____________, je vais très bien _______ je suis heureux.

Hello, I am very well because I am happy.

3. _____________, je vais mal car je suis très __________.

Good evening, I am feeling bad because I am very sad.

4. Salut je vais _______ bien, mais je suis un peu ____________.

Hi, I am quite well, but I am a bit tired.

5. ________, je vais ________ _________ car je suis très ___________.

Hi, I am feeling very bad because I am very annoyed.

	Time 1	Time 2	Time 3	Time 4
Time				
Mistakes				

UNIT 0 – FAST & FURIOUS – Version 2

1. Salut, je _______ bien car je suis ___________.

Hi, I am feeling well because I am relaxed.

2. _____________, je vais très mal car je suis _____________.

Good evening, I am very bad because I am angry.

3. _____________, je vais assez bien car je suis ___________.

Hello, I am feeling quite well because I am happy.

4. Salut je vais ___________, ____________ parce que je suis un peu ___________.

Hi, I am so-so because I am a bit tired.

5. ________, je vais ________ _________ car je suis ___________.

Hi, I am feeling very bad because I am stressed.

	Time 1	Time 2	Time 3	Time 4
Time				
Mistakes				

UNIT 0 – COMMUNICATIVE DRILLS

1	2	3
Hi. My name is Pierre. What is your name? - My name is Dylan. **How are you today, Dylan?** - Today I am well. I am happy. And you?	**Hello. My name is Paul. What is your name?** - My name is Martine. **How are you today, Martine?** - Today I am not well. I am tired and sick. And you?	**Good evening. My name is Suzanne. What is your name?** - My name is Alexandre. **How are you today, Alexandre?** - Today I am very well. I am relaxed. And you?
4	5	6
Good morning. My name is Robert. What is your name? - My name is Irène. **How are you today, Irène?** - Today I am very well. I am very happy. And you?	**Good evening. My name is Béatrice. What is your name?** - My name is Elsa. **How are you today, Elsa?** - Today I am not well. I am very sad. And you?	**Hi. My name is Marc. What is your name?** - My name is Anna. **How are you today, Anna?** - Today I am so-so. I am a bit annoyed. And you?
7	8	9
Hi. My name is Isabelle. What is your name? - My name is Philippe. **How are you today, Philippe?** - Today I am not well. I am very stressed. And you, Isabelle?	**Good evening. My name is Fernand. What is your name?** - My name is Anthony. **How are you today, Anthony?** - Today I am feeling very well. I am very happy. And you?	**Hi. My name is Gabriel. What is your name?** - My name is Lucien. **How are you today, Lucien?** - Today I am so-so because I am a bit tired. And you?

UNIT 0 – COMMUNICATIVE DRILLS
REFEREE CARD

1	2	3
Salut. Je m'appelle Pierre. Comment tu t'appelles? - Je m'appelle Dylan. **Comment ça va aujourd'hui, Dylan?** - Aujourd'hui, je vais bien. Je suis heureux. Et toi?	**Bonjour. Je m'appelle Paul. Comment tu t'appelles?** - Je m'appelle Martine. **Comment ça va aujourd'hui, Martine?** - Aujourd'hui, je ne vais pas bien. Je suis fatiguée et malade. Et toi?	**Bonsoir. Je m'appelle Suzanne. Comment tu t'appelles?** - Je m'appelle Alexandre. **Comment ça va aujourd'hui, Alexandre?** - Aujourd'hui, je vais très bien. Je suis détendu. Et toi?
4	**5**	**6**
Bonjour. Je m'appelle Robert. Comment tu t'appelles? - Je m'appelle Irène. **Comment ça va aujourd'hui, Irène?** - Aujourd'hui, je vais très bien. Je suis très heureuse. Et toi?	**Bonsoir. Je m'appelle Béatrice. Comment tu t'appelles?** - Je m'appelle Elsa. **Comment ça va aujourd'hui, Elsa?** - Aujourd'hui, je ne vais pas bien. Je suis très triste. Et toi?	**Salut. Je m'appelle Marc. Comment tu t'appelles?** - Je m'appelle Anna. **Comment ça va aujourd'hui, Anna?** - Aujourd'hui, je vais comme-ci, comme-ça. Je suis un peu énervée. Et toi?
7	**8**	**9**
Salut. Je m'appelle Isabelle. Comment tu t'appelles? - Je m'appelle Philippe. **Comment ça va aujourd'hui, Philippe?** - Aujourd'hui, je ne vais pas bien. Je suis très stressé. Et toi, Isabelle?	**Bonsoir. Je m'appelle Fernand. Comment tu t'appelles?** - Je m'appelle Anthony. **Comment ça va aujourd'hui, Anthony?** - Je vais très bien. Je suis très heureux. Et toi?	**Salut. Je m'appelle Gabriel. Comment tu t'appelles?** - Je m'appelle Lucien. **Comment ça va aujourd'hui, Lucien?** - Aujourd'hui, je vais comme-ci, comme-ça. Je suis un peu fatigué. Et toi?

UNIT 0 – SURVEY

	What is your name? **Comment tu t'appelles?**	How are you today? **Comment ça va aujourd'hui?**	Why? **Pourquoi?**
e.g.	*Je m'appelle Paul.*	*Aujourd'hui, je vais très bien.*	*Parce que je suis heureux.*
1.			
2.			
3.			
4.			
5.			
6.			
7.			
8.			
9.			

UNIT 0 – ANSWERS

FIND SOMEONE WHO

Find someone who...		Name
1.	...is ill today.	Marc / Louis
2.	...is annoyed.	Léa / Patricia
3.	...is very tired.	Marie-Hélène
4.	...is feeling angry.	Denis
5.	...is feeling very relaxed.	Anne
6.	...is feeling stressed.	Marine
7.	...is feeling well.	Paul
8.	...is feeling happy.	Suzanne / Martine
9.	...is feeling very sad.	Rose
10.	...is feeling very bad.	Pierre / Jules
11.	...is feeling very well.	Charles
12.	...is not sad today	David

STAIRCASE TRANSLATION

Bonjour. Je m'appelle Pierre. Aujourd'hui, je vais très bien parce que je suis heureux et détendu. Comment ça va?

FASTER!

REFEREE SOLUTION

1. Bonjour.
2. Comment ça va?
3. Je vais très bien. Et toi?
4. Merci.
5. Je suis heureux/heureuse et détendu(e).
6. Aujourd'hui, je suis très fatigué(e).
7. Comment tu t'appelles?
8. Je m'appelle Philippe.
9. Aujourd'hui, je suis en colère.
10. Bonne nuit.

FAST & FURIOUS

VERSION 1

1. Salut, je **vais** très bien, mais je suis un **peu** fatigué.

2. **Bonjour**, je vais très bien **car/parce que** je suis heureux.

3. **Bonsoir**, je vais mal car je suis très **triste**.

4. Salut, je vais **assez** bien, mais je suis un peu **fatigué(e)**.

5. **Salut**, je vais **très mal** car je suis très **énervé(e)**.

VERSION 2

1. Salut, je **vais** bien car je suis **détendu(e)**.

2. **Bonsoir**, je vais très mal car je suis **en colère**.

3. **Bonjour**, je vais assez bien car je suis **heureux/heureuse**.

4. Salut je vais **comme-ci, comme-ça** parce que je suis un peu **fatigué(e)**.

5. **Salut**, je vais **très mal** car je suis **stressé(e)**.

UNIT 1
Talking about my age

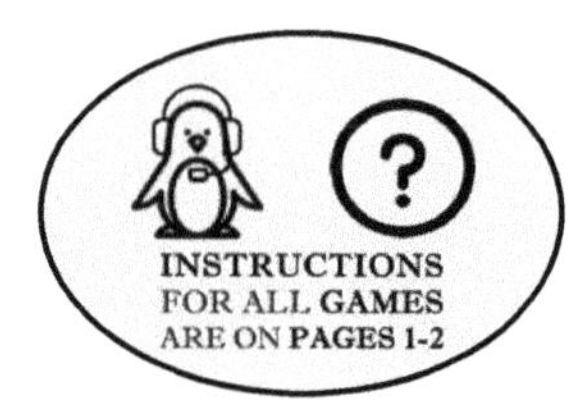

Comment tu t'appelles? *What is your name?*	Quel âge as-tu? *How old are you?*
Comment s'appelle ton frère? *What is your brother's name?*	Quel âge a-t-il? *How old is he?*
Comment s'appelle ta sœur? *What is your sister's name?*	Quel âge a-t-elle? *How old is she?*

Je *I*	m'appelle *am called*			j'ai *I have**	un 1	an *year*
Mon frère *My brother* **Ma sœur** *My sister*	**s'appelle** *is called*	Alexandre Anthony Annabelle Béatrice Charles Denis Émilie Frédéric Isabelle Joséphine Julien Marie Paul Tristan	**et** *and*	**il/elle a** *he/she has**	deux 2 trois 3 quatre 4 cinq 5 six 6 sept 7 huit 8 neuf 9 dix 10 onze 11 douze 12 treize 13 quatorze 14 quinze 15	**ans** *years*

Author's note: in French we use the verb "avoir" [to have] to talk about age
**although "J'ai quatre ans" literally means "I have four years", in English, it's translated as "I am four years old"*

UNIT 1 – FIND SOMEONE WHO – Student Cards

Je m'appelle Marc. J'ai dix ans. **MARC**	Je m'appelle Jules. J'ai six ans. **JULES**	Je m'appelle Marine. J'ai quatorze ans. **MARINE**	Je m'appelle Carla. J'ai quatre ans. **CARLA**
Je m'appelle Léa. J'ai cinq ans. **LÉA**	Je m'appelle Suzanne. J'ai sept ans. **SUZANNE**	Je m'appelle Anne. J'ai huit ans. **ANNE**	Je m'appelle Hélène. J'ai onze ans. **HÉLÈNE**
Je m'appelle Rose. J'ai neuf ans. **ROSE**	Je m'appelle Marie. J'ai quatre ans. **MARIE**	Je m'appelle Pierre. J'ai onze ans. **PIERRE**	Je m'appelle Didier. J'ai neuf ans. **DIDIER**
Je m'appelle Denis. J'ai quinze ans. **DENIS**	Je m'appelle Charles. J'ai treize ans. **CHARLES**	Je m'appelle Patrice. J'ai douze ans. **PATRICE**	Je m'appelle Paul. J'ai huit ans. **PAUL**

UNIT 1 – FIND SOMEONE WHO – Student Grid

Find someone who...		Name
Comment tu t'appelles? *What is your name?* **Quel âge as-tu?** *How old are you?*		
1.	...is twelve.	
2.	...is thirteen.	
3.	...is ten.	
4.	...is eight.	
5.	...is fourteen.	
6.	...is five.	
7.	...is seven.	
8.	...is fifteen.	
9.	...is four.	
10.	...is six.	
11.	...is nine.	
12.	...is eleven.	

UNIT 1 – ORAL PING PONG – Person A

ENGLISH 1	FRENCH 1	ENGLISH 2	FRENCH 2
I am very well today.	Aujourd'hui, je vais très bien.	I am so-so today.	Aujourd'hui, je vais comme-ci, comme-ça.
I am not very well.		I am very well.	
I am fifteen.	J'ai quinze ans.	I am thirteen.	J'ai treize ans.
How old are you?		My brother is twelve.	
My sister is eleven.	Ma sœur a onze ans.	My brother is called Alexandre.	Mon frère s'appelle Alexandre.
How old are you?		My sister is fifteen.	
My sister is called Anne.	Ma sœur s'appelle Anne.	I am eleven.	J'ai onze ans.
My brother is called Denis.		My name is Émilie.	
I am fourteen.	J'ai quatorze ans.	My sister is two.	Ma sœur a deux ans.
I am five.		What is your name?	

UNIT 1 – ORAL PING PONG – Person B

ENGLISH 1	FRENCH 1	ENGLISH 2	FRENCH 2
I am very well today.		I am so-so today.	
I am not very well.	Je ne vais pas très bien.	I am very well.	Je vais très bien.
I am fifteen.		I am thirteen.	
How old are you?	Quel âge as-tu?	My brother is twelve.	Mon frère a douze ans.
My sister is eleven.		My brother is called Alexandre.	
How old are you?	Quel âge as-tu?	My sister is fifteen.	Ma sœur a quinze ans.
My sister is called Anne.		I am eleven.	
My brother is called Denis.	Mon frère s'appelle Denis.	My name is Émilie.	Je m'appelle Émilie.
I am fourteen.		My sister is two.	
I am five.	J'ai cinq ans.	What is your name?	Comment tu t'appelles?

No Snakes No Ladders

7 My brother is called Paul.	8 My brother is twelve.	23 How old is your brother?	24 I am six.
6 I am six.	9 My sister is called Marie.	22 What is your name?	25 I am fifteen.
5 I am fifteen.	10 I am fourteen.	21 How old are you?	26 How are you?
4 How old is your brother?	11 How are you?	20 I am seven.	27 How old is your brother?
3 What is your name?	12 Good evening.	19 How old is your sister?	28 My brother is fourteen.
2 How old are you?	13 What is your name?	18 How old are you?	29 I am ten.
1 Hello.	14 How old are you?	17 My sister is eleven.	30 I am nine.
START	15 I am fourteen.	16 My sister is called Anne.	FINISH

No Snakes No Ladders

7 Mon frère s'appelle Paul.	**8** Mon frère a douze ans.	**23** Quel âge a ton frère?	**24** J'ai six ans.
6 J'ai six ans.	**9** Ma sœur s'appelle Marie.	**22** Comment tu t'appelles?	**25** J'ai quinze ans.
5 J'ai quinze ans.	**10** J'ai quatorze ans.	**21** Quel âge as-tu?	**26** Comment ça va?
4 Quel âge a ton frère?	**11** Comment ça va?	**20** J'ai sept ans.	**27** Quel âge a ton frère?
3 Comment tu t'appelles?	**12** Bonsoir.	**19** Quel âge a ta sœur?	**28** Mon frère a quatorze ans.
2 Quel âge as-tu?	**13** Comment tu t'appelles?	**18** Quel âge as-tu?	**29** J'ai dix ans.
1 Bonjour.	**14** Quel âge as-tu?	**17** Ma sœur a onze ans.	**30** J'ai neuf ans.
DÉPART	**15** J'ai quatorze ans.	**16** Ma sœur s'appelle Anne.	ARRIVÉE

UNIT 1 – STAIRCASE TRANSLATION

Hello.

Hello. How are you?

Hello. How are you? My name is Paul.

Hello. How are you? My name is Paul. I am 15.

Hello. How are you? My name is Paul. I am 15. My sister is called Anne...

* Hello. How are you? My name is Paul. I am 15. My sister is called Anne and she is fourteen.

* Translate the
last step here:

⏱ UNIT 1 – FASTER! 🚀

Say:

1. My name is Charles.
2. Today, I am feeling very well.
3. I am twelve.
4. My sister is called Hélène.
5. My brother is called Robert.
6. Hélène is fourteen.
7. Robert is nine.
8. How are you?
9. What is your name?
10. How old are you?

	Time	Mistakes	Referee's name
1			
2			
3			
4			

UNIT 1 – COMMUNICATIVE DRILLS

1	2	3
What is your name? - My name is Charles. **How are you today, Charles?** - Very well. I am happy. **How old are you?** - I am twelve. And you? **I am thirteen.**	**What is your name?** - My name is Alexandre. **How are you today, Alexandre?** - I am so-so. I am a bit tired. **How old are you?** - I am thirteen. And you? **I am eleven.**	**What is your name?** - My name is Marine. **How are you today, Marine?** - I am well but I am a bit tired. **How old are you?** - I am ten. And you? **I am fourteen.**
4	**5**	**6**
What is your name? - My name is Julien. **How old are you?** - I am fifteen **What is your brother's name?** - His name is Philippe. **How old is your brother?** - He is ten. How old are you?	**What is your name?** - My name is Anne. **How old are you?** - I am thirteen. **What is your sister's name?** - Her name is Caroline. **How old is your sister?** - She is eight. How old are you?	**What is your name?** - My name is Pierre. **How old are you?** - I am eight. **What is your brother's name?** - His name is Raphaël. **How old is your brother?** - He is fourteen.
7	**8**	**9**
Hi. My name is Cyril. I am fifteen. What is your name? - Hi. My name is Suzanne. How are you today, Cyril? **I am well. I am quite relaxed. And you?** - I am so-so. I am a bit tired.	**Hi. My name is Lorène. I am ten. What is your name?** - Hi. My name is Carla. How are you today, Lorène? **I am very well. I am very happy. And you?** - I am so-so. I am a bit sad.	**Hi. My name is Andréa. I am twelve. What is your name?** - Hi. My name is Serge. How are you today, Andréa? **I am not well. I am a bit ill. And you?** - I am well. I am a bit tired, but well.

UNIT 1 – COMMUNICATIVE DRILLS
REFEREE CARD

1	2	3
Comment tu t'appelles? - Je m'appelle Charles. **Comment ça va aujourd'hui Charles?** - Très bien. Je suis heureux. **Quel âge as-tu?** - J'ai douze ans. Et toi? **J'ai treize ans.**	**Comment tu t'appelles?** - Je m'appelle Alexandre. **Comment ça va aujourd'hui, Alexandre?** - Je vais comme-ci, comme-ça. Je suis un peu fatigué. **Quel âge as-tu?** - J'ai treize ans. Et toi? **J'ai onze ans.**	**Comment tu t'appelles?** - Je m'appelle Marine. **Comment ça va aujourd'hui, Marine?** - Je vais bien mais je suis un peu fatiguée. **Quel âge as-tu?** - J'ai dix ans. Et toi? **J'ai quatorze ans.**
4	**5**	**6**
Comment tu t'appelles? - Je m'appelle Julien. **Quel âge as-tu?** - J'ai quinze ans. **Comment s'appelle ton frère?** - Il s'appelle Philippe. **Quel âge a ton frère?** - Il a dix ans. Quel âge as-tu?	**Comment tu t'appelles?** - Je m'appelle Anne. **Quel âge as-tu?** - J'ai treize ans. **Comment s'appelle ta sœur?** - Elle s'appelle Caroline. **Quel âge a ta sœur?** - Elle a huit ans. Quel âge as-tu?	**Comment tu t'appelles?** - Je m'appelle Pierre. **Quel âge as-tu?** - J'ai huit ans. **Comment s'appelle ton frère?** - Il s'appelle Raphaël. **Quel âge a ton frère?** - Il a quatorze ans.
7	**8**	**9**
Salut. Je m'appelle Cyril. J'ai quinze ans. Comment tu t'appelles? - Salut. Je m'appelle Suzanne. Comment ça va aujourd'hui, Cyril? **Je vais bien. Je suis assez détendu. Et toi?** - Je vais comme-ci, comme-ça. Je suis un peu fatiguée.	**Salut. Je m'appelle Lorène. J'ai dix ans. Comment tu t'appelles?** - Salut. Je m'appelle Caroline. Comment ça va aujourd'hui, Lorène? **Je vais très bien. Je suis très heureuse. Et toi?** - Je vais comme-ci, comme-ça. Je suis un peu triste.	**Salut. Je m'appelle Andréa. J'ai douze ans. Comment tu t'appelles?** - Salut. Je m'appelle Serge. Comment ça va aujourd'hui, Andréa? **Je ne vais pas bien. Je suis un peu malade. Et toi?** - Je vais bien. Je suis un peu fatigué, mais bien.

UNIT 1 – SURVEY

	What is your name?	How old are you?	What are your brothers and sisters called?	How old is...?	How old is...?
	Comment tu t'appelles?	**Quel âge as-tu?**	**Comment s'appellent tes frères et sœurs?**	**Quel âge a...?**	**Quel âge a...?**
e.g.	*Je m'appelle Pierre.*	*J'ai onze ans.*	*Mon frère s'appelle Paul et ma sœur s'appelle Carmen.*	*Carmen a seize ans.*	*Paul a quinze ans.*
1.					
2.					
3.					
4.					
5.					
6.					
7.					

UNIT 1 – ANSWERS

FIND SOMEONE WHO

Find someone who...		Name
1.	...is twelve	Patrice
2.	...is thirteen	Charles
3.	...is ten	Marc
4.	...is eight	Anne / Paul
5.	...is fourteen	Marine
6.	...is five	Léa
7.	...is seven	Suzanne
8.	...is fifteen	Denis
9.	...is four	Carla / Marie
10.	...is six	Jules
11.	...is nine	Didier / Rose
12.	...is eleven	Hélène / Pierre

STAIRCASE TRANSLATION

Bonjour. Comment ça va? Je m'appelle Paul. J'ai quinze ans. Ma sœur s'appelle Anne et elle a quatorze ans.

FASTER!

REFEREE SOLUTION:
1. Je m'appelle Charles.
2. Aujourd'hui, je vais très bien.
3. J'ai douze ans.
4. Ma sœur s'appelle Hélène.
5. Mon frère s'appelle Robert.
6. Hélène a quatorze ans.
7. Robert a neuf ans.
8. Comment ça va?
9. Comment tu t'appelles?
10. Quel âge as-tu?

UNIT 2
Saying when my birthday is

Comment tu t'appelles? *What is your name?* **D'où es-tu?** *Where are you from?* **Quel âge as-tu?** *How old are you?* **Quelle est la date de ton anniversaire?** *When is your birthday?*				**Comment s'appelle ton ami(e)?** *What is your friend's name?* **D'où est-il/est-elle?** **Quel âge a-t-il/a-t-elle?** *How old is he/she?* **Quelle est la date de son anniversaire?** *When is his/her birthday?*	
Je m'appelle Julien *I am called Julien*	**je suis de Paris** *I am from Paris* ***j'ai X ans** *I am X years old*		**mon anniversaire est le** *my birthday is the*	1 premier *first* 2 deux 3 trois 4 quatre 5 cinq 6 six 7 sept 8 huit 9 neuf 10 dix 11 onze 12 douze 13 treize	**janvier** *January* **février** **mars** **avril** **mai**
Mon amie s'appelle Catherine *My friend is called Catherine* **Mon ami s'appelle Francis** *My friend is called Francis*	**il/elle est de Biarritz** *he/she is from Biarritz* ***il/elle a X ans** *he/she is X years old*	**et** *and*	**son anniversaire est le** *his/her birthday is the*	14 quatorze 15 quinze 16 seize 17 dix-sept 18 dix-huit 19 dix-neuf 20 vingt 21 vingt-et-un 22 vingt-deux 23 vingt-trois 24 vingt-quatre 25 vingt-cinq 26 vingt-six 27 vingt-sept 28 vingt-huit 29 vingt-neuf 30 trente 31 trente-et-un	**juin** **juillet** **août** **septembre** **octobre** **novembre** **décembre**

*AUTHOR'S NOTE: *J'ai or il/elle a actually means "I have" and "he/she has" in French. You use this verb for telling age. You will see it many times throughout this booklet! ☺*

UNIT 2 – FIND SOMEONE WHO – Student Cards

Je m'appelle Sophie. Mon anniversaire est le douze mars. **SOPHIE**	Je m'appelle Camille. Mon anniversaire est le quinze juin. **CAMILLE**	Je m'appelle Matéo. Mon anniversaire est le treize avril. **MATÉO**	Je m'appelle Alexandre. Mon anniversaire est le treize septembre. **ALEXANDRE**
Je m'appelle Valentine. Mon anniversaire est le trente décembre. **VALENTINE**	Je m'appelle Anna. Mon anniversaire est le cinq février. **ANNA**	Je m'appelle Sylvain. Mon anniversaire est le premier novembre. **SYLVAIN**	Je m'appelle Éric. Mon anniversaire est le trois mai. **ÉRIC**
Je m'appelle Isabelle. Mon anniversaire est le quatre août. **ISABELLE**	Je m'appelle Daniel. Mon anniversaire est le dix-sept mai. **DANIEL**	Je m'appelle Léonard. Mon anniversaire est le seize octobre. **LÉONARD**	Je m'appelle Philippe. Mon anniversaire est le six août. **PHILIPPE**
Je m'appelle Marie. Mon anniversaire est le quatorze février. **MARIE**	Je m'appelle Lucas. Mon anniversaire est le douze janvier. **LUCAS**	Je m'appelle Sébastien. Mon anniversaire est le treize juillet. **SÉBASTIEN**	Je m'appelle Paul. Mon anniversaire est le onze octobre. **PAUL**

UNIT 2 – FIND SOMEONE WHO – Student Grid

Find someone whose birthday is in...		Name(s)
1.	...January	
2.	...February	
3.	... March	
4.	...April	
5.	...May	
6.	...June	
7.	...July	
8.	...August	
9.	...September	
10.	...October	
11.	...November	
12.	...December	

UNIT 2 – ORAL PING PONG – Person A

ENGLISH 1	FRENCH 1	ENGLISH 2	FRENCH 2
I am from Paris.	Je suis de Paris.	My birthday is on 20th October.	Mon anniversaire est le vingt octobre.
I am not very well.		When is your birthday?	
My male friend is called Samuel.	Mon ami s'appelle Samuel.	I am 13. My birthday is on 6th June.	J'ai treize ans. Mon anniversaire est le six juin.
How old are you?		My brother is 12. His birthday is on 13th April.	
My female friend is called Catherine.	Mon amie s'appelle Catherine.	My friend is 15. Her birthday is on 20th June.	Mon amie a quinze ans. Son anniversaire est le 20 juin.
When is your birthday?		My brother is 10. His birthday is on 15th August.	
My birthday is on 5th May.	Mon anniversaire est le cinq mai.	I am eleven. My birthday is on 31st May.	J'ai onze ans. Mon anniversaire est le trente-et-un mai.
His birthday is on 11th March.		I am 6. My birthday is on 19th September.	
I am from Biarritz.	Je suis de Biarritz.	I am 9. My birthday is on 21st July.	J'ai neuf ans. Mon anniversaire est le vingt-et-un juillet.
My birthday is on 15th June.		When is his/her birthday?	

UNIT 2 – ORAL PING PONG – Person B

ENGLISH 1	FRENCH 1	ENGLISH 2	FRENCH 2
I am from Paris.		**My birthday is on 20th October.**	
I am not very well.	Je ne vais pas très bien.	**When is your birthday?**	Quelle est la date de ton anniversaire?
My male friend is called Samuel.		**I am 13. My birthday is on 6th June.**	
How old are you?	Quel âge as-tu?	**My brother is 12. His birthday is on 13th April.**	Mon frère a douze ans. Son anniversaire est le treize avril.
My female friend is called Catherine.		**My friend is 15. Her birthday is on 20th June.**	
When is your birthday?	Quelle est la date de ton anniversaire?	**My brother is 10. His birthday is on 15th August.**	Mon frère a dix ans. Son anniversaire est le quinze août.
My birthday is on 5th May.		**I am eleven. My birthday is on 31st May.**	
His birthday is on 11th March.	Son anniversaire est le onze mars.	**I am 6. My birthday is on 19th September.**	J'ai six ans. Mon anniversaire est le dix-neuf septembre.
I am from Biarritz.		**I am 9. My birthday is on 21st July.**	
My birthday is on 15th June.	Mon anniversaire est le quinze juin.	**When is his/her birthday?**	Quelle est la date de son anniversaire?

No Snakes No Ladders

START	1 How old are you?	2 I am eleven.	3 Where are you from?	4 I am from Paris.	5 My birthday is on 20th June.	6 My birthday is on 15th August.	7 My birthday is on 29th May.
15 His birthday is on 1st February.	14 Her birthday is on 16th January.	13 How old are you?	12 When is her birthday?	11 When is your birthday?	10 My birthday is on 15th May.	9 My birthday is on 13th September.	8 My birthday is on 31st July.
16 I am 9 and my birthday is on 17th May.	17 I am 13 and my birthday is on 10th March.	18 I am 17 and my birthday is on 30th April.	19 I am 12 and my birthday is on 15th August.	20 I am 7 and my birthday is on 20th December.	21 How old are you?	22 What is your name?	23 How old is your friend?
FINISH	30 I am 17 and my birthday is on 8th December.	29 I am 10 and my birthday is on 13th October.	28 I am 15 and my birthday is on 8th June.	27 I am 30 and my birthday is on 2nd January.	26 I am 20 and my birthday is on 12th April.	25 Where are you from?	24 When is your birthday?

No Snakes No Ladders

DÉPART	1 Quel âge as-tu?	2 J'ai onze ans.	3 D'où es-tu?	4 Je suis de Paris.	5 Mon anniversaire est le vingt juin.	6 Mon anniversaire est le quinze août.	7 Mon anniversaire est le vingt-neuf mai.
15 Son anniversaire est le premier février.	14 Son anniversaire est le seize janvier.	13 Quel âge as-tu?	12 Quelle est la date de son anniversaire?	11 Quelle est la date de ton anniversaire?	10 Mon anniversaire est le quinze mai.	9 Mon anniversaire est le treize septembre.	8 Mon anniversaire est le trente-et-un juillet.
16 J'ai neuf ans et mon anniversaire est le dix-sept mai.	17 J'ai treize ans et mon anniversaire est le dix mars.	18 J'ai dix-sept ans et mon anniversaire est le trente avril.	19 J'ai douze ans et mon anniversaire est le quinze août.	20 J'ai sept ans et mon anniversaire est le vingt décembre.	21 Quel âge as-tu?	22 Comment tu t'appelles?	23 Quel âge a ton ami?
ARRIVÉE	30 J'ai dix-sept ans et mon anniversaire est le huit décembre.	29 J'ai dix ans et mon anniversaire est le treize octobre.	28 J'ai quinze ans et mon anniversaire est le huit juin.	27 J'ai trente ans et mon anniversaire est le deux janvier.	26 J'ai vingt ans et mon anniversaire est le douze avril.	25 D'où es-tu?	24 Quelle est la date de ton anniversaire?

UNIT 2 – STAIRCASE TRANSLATION

Hello. How are you?

Hello. How are you? My name is Jules.

Hello. How are you? My name is Jules. I am from Paris.

Hello. How are you? My name is Jules. I am from Paris. I am 11.

Hello. How are you? My name is Jules. I am from Paris. I am 11. My birthday is on 31st January. And you?

* Hello how are you? My name is Jules. I am from Paris. I am 11. My birthday is on 31st January. And you? What is your name? Where are you from? How old are you? When is your birthday?

* Translate the
last step here:

 UNIT 2 – FASTER!

Say:

1. My name is Charles.
2. Today I am well.
3. I am eleven.
4. I am from Paris.
5. My birthday is on 20th June.
6. I have a brother, Robert.
7. Robert is nine.
8. His birthday is on 10th July.
9. How are you?
10. How old are you?
11. Where are you from?
12. When is your birthday?

	Time	Mistakes	Referee's name
1			
2			
3			
4			

THE LANGUAGE GYM
SPEAKING BOOKLET I

UNIT 2 – TRAPDOOR – Version 1

Anna Catherine Denis Francis Marine Paul Suzanne	a	deux trois cinq huit dix	onze douze treize quatorze quinze	ans.	Son anniversaire est le	deux trois cinq sept neuf onze seize vingt	janvier. février. mars. juin. juillet. août. octobre. décembre.

1. Anna is five years old. Her birthday is on 3rd July.
2. Denis is fifteen years old. His birthday is on 16th December.
3. Paul is eight years old. His birthday is on 2nd August.
4. Marine is thirteen years old. Her birthday is on 20th January.
5. Suzanne is three years old. Her birthday is on 7th June.
6. Catherine is ten years old. Her birthday is on 9th March.
7. Francis is twelve years old. His birthday is on 11th October.

	Time 1	Time 2	Time 3	Time 4
Time				
Mistakes				

UNIT 2 – TRAPDOOR – Version 2

Alexandre Andréa Cassandra Daniel Louise Patrice Patricia	a	deux trois quatre six sept	neuf onze treize quatorze quinze	ans.	Son anniversaire est le	quatre six huit dix quinze seize vingt-et-un trente	janvier. février. avril. juin. juillet. août. septembre. novembre.

1. Alexandre is eleven years old. His birthday is on 6th April.
2. Andréa is nine years old. Her birthday is on 10th September.
3. Cassandra is fourteen years old. Her birthday is on 21st January.
4. Daniel is six years old. His birthday is on 16th November.
5. Louise is fifteen years old. Her birthday is on 8th February.
6. Patrice is seven years old. His birthday is on 4th August.
7. Patricia is eleven years old. Her birthday is on 30th September.

	Time 1	Time 2	Time 3	Time 4
Time				
Mistakes				

UNIT 2 – COMMUNICATIVE DRILLS

1	2	3
What is your name?	**What is your name?**	**What is your name?**
- My name is Martine.	- My name is Suzanne.	- My name is Sonia.
Where are you from?	**Where are you from?**	**Where are you from?**
- I am from Paris.	- I am from Biarritz.	- I am from Valence.
How old are you?	**How old are you?**	**How old are you?**
- I am ten.	- I am thirteen.	- I am sixteen.
When is your birthday?	**When is your birthday?**	**When is your birthday?**
- My birthday is on 15th August.	- My birthday is on 20th June.	- My birthday is on 1st January.
4	**5**	**6**
What is your name?	**What is your name?**	**What is your name?**
- My name is Phlippe.	- My name is Alexandre.	- My name is Stéphanie.
Where are you from?	**Where are you from?**	**Where are you from?**
- I am from Briançon.	- I am from Grenoble.	- I am from Monaco.
How old are you?	**How old are you?**	**How old are you?**
- I am twelve.	- I am eleven.	- I am nine.
When is your birthday?	**When is your birthday?**	**When is your birthday?**
- My birthday is on 21st July.	- My birthday is on 16th September.	- My birthday is on 11th June.
7	**8**	**9**
What is your name?	**What is your name?**	**What is your name?**
- My name is Julien.	- My name is Samuel.	- My name is Marie.
Where are you from?	**Where are you from?**	**Where are you from?**
- I am from Cannes.	- I am from Tours.	- I am from Saint-Étienne.
How old are you?	**How old are you?**	**How old are you?**
- I am eight.	- I am thirteen.	- I am twenty seven.
When is your birthday?	**When is your birthday?**	**When is your birthday?**
- My birthday is on 19th October.	- My birthday is on 18th May.	- My birthday is on 5th April.

UNIT 2 - COMMUNICATIVE DRILLS
REFEREE CARD

1	2	3
Comment tu t'appelles?	**Comment tu t'appelles?**	**Comment tu t'appelles?**
- Je m'appelle Martine.	- Je m'appelle Suzanne	- Je m'appelle Sonia.
D'où es-tu?	**D'où es-tu?**	**D'où es-tu?**
- Je suis de Paris.	- Je suis de Biarritz.	- Je suis de Valence.
Quel âge as-tu?	**Quel âge as-tu?**	**Quel âge as-tu?**
- J'ai dix ans.	- J'ai treize ans.	- J'ai seize ans.
Quelle est la date de ton anniversaire?	**Quelle est la date de ton anniversaire?**	**Quelle est la date de ton anniversaire?**
- Mon anniversaire est le quinze août.	- Mon anniversaire est le vingt juin.	- Mon anniversaire est le premier janvier.

4	5	6
Comment tu t'appelles?	**Comment tu t'appelles?**	**Comment tu t'appelles?**
- Je m'appelle Philippe.	- Je m'appelle Alexandre.	- Je m'appelle Stéphanie.
D'où es-tu?	**D'où es-tu?**	**D'où es-tu?**
- Je suis de Briançon.	- Je suis de Grenoble.	- Je suis de Monaco.
Quel âge as-tu?	**Quel âge as-tu?**	**Quel âge as-tu?**
- J'ai douze ans.	- J'ai onze ans.	- J'ai neuf ans.
Quelle est la date de ton anniversaire?	**Quelle est la date de ton anniversaire?**	**Quelle est la date de ton anniversaire?**
- Mon anniversaire est le vingt-et-un juin.	- Mon anniversaire est le seize septembre.	- Mon anniversaire est le onze juin.

7	8	9
Comment tu t'appelles?	**Comment tu t'appelles?**	**Comment tu t'appelles?**
- Je m'appelle Julien.	- Je m'appelle Samuel.	- Je m'appelle Marie.
D'où es-tu?	**D'où es-tu?**	**D'où es-tu?**
- Je suis de Cannes.	- Je suis de Tours.	- Je suis de Saint-Étienne.
Quel âge as-tu?	**Quel âge as-tu?**	**Quel âge as-tu?**
- J'ai huit ans.	- J'ai treize ans.	- J'ai vingt-sept ans
Quelle est la date de ton anniversaire?	**Quelle est la date de ton anniversaire?**	**Quelle est la date de ton anniversaire?**
- Mon anniversaire est le dix-neuf octobre.	- Mon anniversaire est le dix-huit mai.	- Mon anniversaire est le cinq avril.

UNIT 2 – SURVEY

	What is your name?	How are you today?	How old are you?	When is your birthday?	Where are you from?
	Comment tu t'appelles?	**Comment ça va aujourd'hui?**	**Quel âge as-tu?**	**Quelle est la date de ton anniversaire?**	**D'où es-tu?**
e.g.	*Je m'appelle Suzanne.*	*Je vais très bien, merci.*	*J'ai dix ans.*	*Mon anniversaire est le cinq mai.*	*Je suis de Biarritz.*
1.					
2.					
3.					
4.					
5.					
6.					
7.					

UNIT 2 – ANSWERS

FIND SOMEONE WHO

Find someone whose birthday is in...	Name(s)
1. ...January	Lucas
2. ...February	Marie / Anna
3. ... Mars	Sophie
4. ...April	Matéo
5. ...May	Éric / Daniel
6. ...June	Camille
7. ...July	Sébastien
8. ...August	Philippe / Isabelle
9. ...September	Alexandre
10. ...October	Paul / Léonard
11. ...November	Sylvain
12. ...December	Valentine

STAIRCASE TRANSLATION

Bonjour. Comment ça va? Je m'appelle Jules. Je suis de Paris. J'ai onze ans. Mon anniversaire est le trente-et-un janvier. Et toi? Comment tu t'appelles? D'où es-tu? Quel âge as-tu? Quelle est la date de ton anniversaire?

FASTER!

REFEREE SOLUTION:

1. Je m'appelle Charles.
2. Aujourd'hui, je vais bien.
3. J'ai onze ans.
4. Je suis de Paris.
5. Mon anniversaire est le vingt juin.
6. J'ai un frère, Robert.
7. Robert a neuf ans.
8. Son anniversaire est le dix juillet.
9. Comment ça va?
10. Quel âge as-tu?
11. D'où es-tu?
12. Quelle est la date de ton anniversaire?

TRAPDOOR

VERSION 1

1. Anna a cinq ans. Son anniversaire est le trois juillet.
2. Denis a quinze ans. Son anniversaire est le seize décembre.
3. Paul a huit ans. Son anniversaire est le deux août.
4. Marine a treize ans. Son anniversaire est le vingt janvier.
5. Suzanne a trois ans. Son anniversaire est le sept juin.
6. Catherine a dix ans. Son anniversaire est le neuf mars.
7. Francis a douze ans. Son anniversaire est le onze octobre.

VERSION 2

1. Alexandre a onze ans. Son anniversaire est le six avril.
2. Andréa a neuf ans. Son anniversaire est le dix septembre.
3. Cassandra a quatorze ans. Son anniversaire est le vingt-et-un janvier.
4. Daniel a six ans. Son anniversaire est le seize novembre.
5. Louise a quinze ans. Son anniversaire est le huit février.
6. Patrice a sept ans. Son anniversaire est le quatre août.
7. Patricia a onze ans. Son anniversaire est le trente septembre.

UNIT 3
Saying where I live and am from

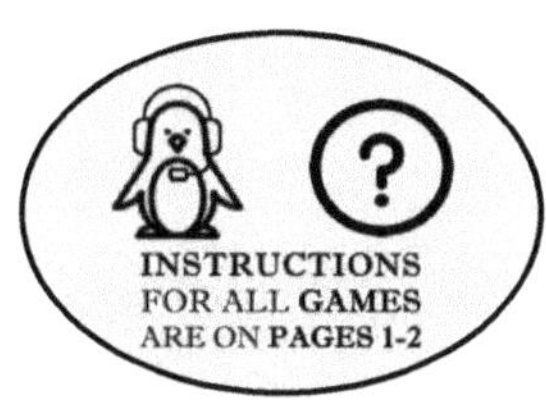

Où habites-tu?		*Where do you live?*			
D'où es-tu?		*Where are you from?*			

	je vis dans *I live in* **j'habite dans** *I live in*	**une** *a*	**belle** *beautiful* **grande** *big* **jolie** *pretty* **petite** *small*	**maison** *house*	**dans le centre** *in the centre*
		un appartement *a flat*	**dans un bâtiment ancien** *in an old building* **dans un bâtiment moderne** *in a modern building* **dans un bâtiment neuf** *in a new building*		**dans la banlieue** *on the outskirts* **sur la côte** *on the coast*
Je m'appelle David et… *My name is David and…*	**je suis de** *I am from*	**Biarritz**	**dans le Pays basque** *southwest region of France*		
		Brest	**en Bretagne (en France)** *northwest of France*		
		Bruxelles	**en Belgique (la capitale)** *capital of Belgium*		
		Casablanca	**au Maroc (sur la côte)** *coast of Morocco*		
		Dakar	**au Sénégal (la capitale)** *capital of Senegal*		
		Fort-de-France	**en Martinique (la capitale)** *capital of Martinique*		
		Libreville	**au Gabon (la capitale)** *capital of Gabon*		
		Montréal	**au Québec** *Quebec, Canadian province*		
		Nice	**en Provence (en France)** *southeast of France*		
		Nouméa	**en Nouvelle Calédonie** *New Caledonia*		
		Paris	**en France (la capitale)** *capital of France*		
		Saint-Denis	**à la Réunion (la capitale)** *capital of Reunion Island*		
		Strasbourg	**en Alsace (en France)** *northeast region of France*		

UNIT 3 – FIND SOMEONE WHO – Student Cards

J'habite dans une jolie maison dans le centre de Cannes. **EMMANUEL**	J'habite dans une petite maison dans le centre de Marmande. **ANDRÉ**	J'habite dans un bâtiment moderne sur la côte, en Bretagne. **LUCIE**	J'habite dans une grande maison dans la banlieue de Bayonne. **MICHEL**
J'habite dans un grand appartement à Paris. **ALEXANDRE**	J'habite dans une très petite maison à Quimper. **THOMAS**	J'habite dans une petite maison dans la banlieue de Montréal. **MARTINE**	J'habite dans un petit appartement sur la côte à Nice. **DIDIER**
J'habite dans une jolie maison sur la côte près de Narbonne. **JULIEN**	J'habite dans une petite maison à Papeete à Tahiti. **NATHALIE**	J'habite dans un grand appartement dans un bâtiment ancien. **GABRIELLE**	J'habite dans une très petite maison à Toulouse. **DENISE**
J'habite dans un appartement dans la banlieue de Marseille. **RAPHAËL**	J'habite dans une grande maison moderne à Biarritz, dans le Pays basque. **ADRIENNE**	J'habite dans une grande et jolie maison dans le centre de Briançon. **VICTOIRE**	J'habite dans une belle maison dans la banlieue de Valence, en France. **MARCEL**

UNIT 3 – FIND SOMEONE WHO – Student Grid

Find someone who...		Name(s)
Comment tu t'appelles?	*What is your name?*	
Où habites-tu?	*Where do you live?*	
Comment est ta maison?	*What is your house like?*	
1.	...lives in a big and pretty house.	
2.	...lives in a very small house.	
3.	...lives in a small flat on the coast.	
4.	...lives in the Basque Country	
5.	...lives in an small house in the centre of town.	
6.	...lives in an old building.	
7.	...lives in a big flat in the capital city of France.	
8.	...lives in Cannes.	
9.	...lives in a small house in Tahiti.	
10.	...lives near Narbonne.	
11.	...lives in a modern building.	
12.	...lives on the outskirts of their city.	

UNIT 3 – ORAL PING PONG – Person A

ENGLISH 1	FRENCH 1	ENGLISH 2	FRENCH 2
What is your name?	Comment tu t'appelles?	I live in a flat.	J'habite dans un appartement.
My name is David.		I live in a house.	
Where do you live?	Où habites-tu?	I live in a big house.	J'habite dans une grande maison.
Where are you from?		I live in a beautiful house.	
I am from Cannes.	Je suis de Cannes.	I live in an old building.	J'habite dans un bâtiment ancien.
I am from France.		I live in a modern building.	
I am from Monaco.	Je suis de Monaco.	I live in a small house.	J'habite dans une petite maison.
I am from the capital of Germany.		I live in a pretty house.	
I live in Biarritz.	J'habite à Biarritz.	I live in a house on the outskirts.	J'habite dans une maison dans la banlieue.
I live in a flat on the coast.		I live in a flat in the centre.	

UNIT 3 – ORAL PING PONG – Person B

ENGLISH 1	FRENCH 1	ENGLISH 2	FRENCH 2
What is your name?		I live in a flat.	
My name is David.	Je m'appelle David.	I live in a house.	J'habite dans une maison.
Where do you live?		I live in a big house.	
Where are you from?	D'où es-tu?	I live in a beautiful house.	J'habite dans une belle maison.
I am from Cannes.		I live in an old building.	
I am from France.	Je suis de France.	I live in a modern building.	J'habite dans un bâtiment moderne.
I am from Monaco.		I live in a small house.	
I am from the capital of Germany.	Je suis de la capitale de l'Allemagne.	I live in a pretty house.	J'habite dans une jolie maison.
I live in Biarritz.		I live in a house on the outskirts.	
I live in a house on the coast.	J'habite dans une maison sur la côte.	I live in a flat in the centre.	J'habite dans un appartement dans le centre.

No Snakes No Ladders

7 I am twelve and I am from Nice.	**6** I am from the capital of Germany.	**5** I am from Paris.	**4** I am from France.	**3** I am from England.	**2** Where are you from?	**1** What is your name? START
8 I am 13 and am from Calais.	**9** Where are you from?	**10** Where do you live?	**11** I live in a house.	**12** I live in a flat.	**13** How old are you?	**14** When is your birthday?
23 My name is Paul. I am 12 and I live in Chamonix in France.	**22** I am 17. I am from Paris. I live in a flat in the centre.	**21** How old are you?	**20** Where do you live?	**19** Where are you from?	**18** I am from Biarritz. I live in a big house on the outskirts.	**17** I am from Calais. I live in a small house on the coast.
24 I am 18. I live in a small flat on the outskirts.	**25** I am 16. I live in an old building in the centre.	**26** Where are you from? Where do you live?	**27** I am 19. I live in a pretty house on the coast.	**28** I am 11. I live in a big house in a modern building.	**29** I am 11. I live in Bastia in a big house in the centre.	**30** I am 14. I live in Toulouse in a big flat. FINISH
					15 I am 17. I live in Cannes.	**16** I am 10. I live in a big house in Annecy.

No Snakes No Ladders

1 — Comment tu t'appelles?

2 — D'où es-tu?

3 — Je suis d'Angleterre.

4 — Je suis de France.

5 — Je suis de Paris.

6 — Je suis de la capitale de l'Allemagne.

7 — J'ai douze ans et je suis de Nice.

8 — J'ai treize ans et je suis de Calais.

9 — D'où es-tu?

10 — Où habites-tu?

11 — J'habite dans une maison.

12 — J'habite dans un appartement.

13 — Quel âge as-tu?

14 — Quelle est la date de ton anniversaire?

DÉPART — **15** — J'ai dix-sept ans. J'habite à Cannes.

16 — J'ai dix ans. J'habite dans une grande maison à Annecy.

17 — Je suis de Calais. J'habite dans une petite maison sur la côte.

18 — Je suis de Biarritz. J'habite dans une grande maison dans la banlieue.

19 — D'où es-tu?

20 — Où habites-tu?

21 — Quel âge as-tu?

22 — J'ai dix-sept ans. Je suis de Paris. J'habite dans un appartement dans le centre.

23 — Je m'appelle Paul. J'ai douze ans et j'habite à Chamonix en France.

24 — J'ai dix-huit ans. J'habite dans un petit appartement dans la banlieue.

25 — J'ai seize ans. J'habite dans un bâtiment ancien dans le centre.

26 — D'où es-tu? Où habites-tu?

27 — J'ai dix-neuf ans. J'habite dans une jolie maison sur la côte.

28 — J'ai onze ans. J'habite dans une grande maison dans un bâtiment moderne.

29 — J'ai onze ans. J'habite à Bastia dans une grande maison dans le centre.

30 — J'ai quatorze ans. J'habite à Toulouse dans un grand appartement.

ARRIVÉE

UNIT 3 – STAIRCASE TRANSLATION

Hi. My name is Jean.

Hi. My name is Jean. I am twelve.

Hi. My name is Jean. I am twelve. I am from Dakar, the capital of Senegal.

Hi. My name is Jean. I am twelve. I am from Dakar, the capital of Senegal. I live in a small house…

Hi. My name is Jean. I am twelve. I am from Dakar, the capital of Senegal. I live in a small house on the outskirts.

* Hi. My name is Jean. I am twelve. I am from Dakar, the capital of Senegal. I live in a small house on the outskirts. And you? How are you? Where are you from? Where do you live?

* Translate the
last step here:

 # UNIT 3 – FASTER! 

Say:

1. I live in a small house.
2. I live in a big and pretty house.
3. I live on the outskirts of Paris.
4. I live in a big house in the centre.
5. I live in a small flat on the coast.
6. I live in a big house in Bayonne.
7. I live in a modern building.
8. I live in an old building.
9. I live in a small and pretty house.
10. I live in a big and pretty flat.

	Time	Mistakes	Referee's name
1			
2			
3			
4			

UNIT 3 – INFORMATION GAP TASK

Use these questions to find out the missing information from your partner.

1. **Quel âge a __________?**   *How old is __________ ?*
2. **Quelle est la date de l'anniversaire de __________?**   *When is __________'s birthday?*
3. **_______ habite dans une maison ou un appartement?**   *Does __________ live in a house or a flat?*
4. **Comment est sa maison/son appartement?**   *What is his house/flat like?*
5. **Dans quelle ville habite __________?**   *What city does __________ live in?*
6. **De quel pays est __________?**   *What country is __________ from?*

PARTNER 1					
Name	**Age**	**Birthday**	**Accommodation**	**City/Town**	**Country**
David	15		Small house	Paris	
Marine		13th June			France
Jean	14		Big flat	Nouméa	
Paul	12	20th August			Germany
Suzanne		1st September	Beautiful house		Senegal

PARTNER 2					
Name	**Age**	**Birthday**	**Accommodation**	**City/Town**	**Country**
David		12th March			France
Marine	9		Small flat	Biarritz	
Jean		9th January			New Caledonia
Paul			Modern house	Berlin	
Suzanne	13			Dakar	

UNIT 3 – COMMUNICATIVE DRILLS

1	2	3
Where are you from? - I am from Biarritz. **Where do you live?** - I live in Bayonne. **Do you live in house or a flat?** - I live in a big house in the centre of Bayonne.	**Where are you from?** - I am from Brussels in Belgium. **Where do you live?** - I live in Paris. **Do you live in house or a flat?** - I live in a big flat on the outskirts of Paris.	**Where are you from?** - I am from Montréal in Québec. **Where do you live?** - I live in Whistler in Canada. **Do you live in house or a flat?** - I live in a small house in the centre.
4	5	6
Where are you from? - I am from Valence in France. **Where do you live?** - I live in Valence. **Do you live in house or a flat?** - I live in a pretty flat in an old building in the centre.	**Where are you from?** - I am from Libreville in Gabon. **Where do you live?** - I live in Bordeaux in France. **Do you live in house or a flat?** - I live in a small flat on the outskirts.	**Where are you from?** - I am from Strasbourg in France. **Where do you live?** - I live in Nantes. **Do you live in house or a flat?** - I live in a small flat in an old building in the centre.
7	8	9
Where are you from? - I am from Granville in France. **Where do you live?** - I live in Nice. **Do you live in a house or a flat?** - I live in a big flat in a modern building in the centre of the city.	**Where are you from?** - I am from Paris in France. **Where do you live?** - I live in Marseille. **Do you live in house or a flat?** - I live in a big and beautiful house on the coast.	**Where are you from?** - I am from Casablanca in Morocco. **Where do you live?** - I live in Marrakesh. **Do you live in house or a flat?** - I live in a small flat on the outskirts of the city.

UNIT 3 – COMMUNICATIVE DRILLS
REFEREE CARD

1	2	3
D'où es-tu? - Je suis de Biarritz. **Où habites-tu?** - J'habite à Bayonne. **Tu habites dans une maison ou un appartement?** - J'habite dans une grande maison dans le centre de Bayonne.	**D'où es-tu?** - Je suis de Bruxelles, en Belgique. **Où habites-tu?** - J'habite à Paris. **Tu habites dans une maison ou un appartement?** - J'habite dans un grand appartement dans la banlieue de Paris.	**D'où es-tu?** - Je suis de Montréal au Québec. **Où habites-tu?** - J'habite à Whistler au Canada. **Tu habites dans une maison ou un appartement?** - J'habite dans une petite maison dans le centre.
4	**5**	**6**
D'où es-tu? - Je suis de Valence en France. **Où habites-tu?** - J'habite à Valence. **Tu habites dans une maison ou un appartement?** - J'habite dans un joli appartement dans un bâtiment ancien dans le centre.	**D'où es-tu?** - Je suis de Libreville au Gabon. **Où habites-tu?** - J'habite à Bordeaux en France. **Tu habites dans une maison ou un appartement?** - J'habite dans un petit appartement dans la banlieue.	**D'où es-tu?** - Je suis de Strasbourg en France. **Où habites-tu?** - J'habite à Nantes. **Tu habites dans une maison ou un appartement?** - J'habite dans un petit appartement dans un bâtiment ancien dans le centre.
7	**8**	**9**
D'où es-tu? - Je suis de Granville en France. **Où habites-tu?** - J'habite à Nice. **Tu habites dans une maison ou un appartement?** - J'habite dans un grand appartement dans un bâtiment moderne dans le centre de la ville.	**D'où es-tu?** - Je suis de Paris en France. **Où habites-tu?** - J'habite à Marseille. **Tu habites dans une maison ou un appartement?** - J'habite dans une grande et belle maison sur la côte.	**D'où es-tu?** - Je suis de Casablanca au Maroc. **Où habites-tu?** - J'habite à Marrakesh. **Tu habites dans une maison ou un appartement?** - J'habite dans un petit appartement dans la banlieue de la ville.

UNIT 3 – SURVEY

	How are you today?	How old are you?	When is your birthday?	Where are you from?	Where do you live?
	Comment ça va aujourd'hui?	**Quel âge as-tu?**	**Quelle est la date de ton anniversaire?**	**D'où es-tu?**	**Où habites-tu?**
e.g.	*Je vais très bien, merci.*	*J'ai douze ans.*	*Mon anniversaire est le quinze mars.*	*Je suis de Bordeaux.*	*J'habite dans une grande maison dans le centre.*
1.					
2.					
3.					
4.					
5.					
6.					
7.					

UNIT 3 – ANSWERS

FIND SOMEONE WHO

	Find someone who...	Name(s)
1.	...lives in a big and pretty house.	Victoire
2.	...lives in a very small house.	Denise / Thomas
3.	...lives in a small flat on the coast.	Didier
4.	...lives in the Basque Country	Adrienne
5.	...lives in an small house in the centre of town.	André
6.	...lives in an old building.	Gabrielle
7.	...lives in a big flat in the capital city of France.	Alexandre
8.	...lives in Cannes.	Emmanuel
9.	...lives in a small house in Tahiti.	Nathalie
10.	...lives near Narbonne.	Julien
11.	...lives in a modern building.	Lucie
12.	...lives on the outskirts of their city.	Marcel / Michel / Martine / Raphaël

STAIRCASE TRANSLATION

Salut. Je m'appelle Jean. J'ai douze ans. Je suis de Dakar, la capitale du Sénégal. J'habite dans une petite maison dans la banlieue. Et toi? Comment ça va? D'où es-tu? Où habites-tu?

FASTER!

REFEREE SOLUTION:

1. J'habite dans une petite maison.
2. J'habite dans une grande et jolie maison.
3. J'habite dans la banlieue de Paris.
4. J'habite dans une grande maison dans le centre.
5. J'habite dans un petit appartement sur la côte.
6. J'habite dans une grande maison à Bayonne.
7. J'habite dans un bâtiment moderne.
8. J'habite dans un bâtiment ancien.
9. J'habite dans une petite et jolie maison.
10. J'habite dans un grand et joli appartement.

INFORMATION GAP TASK

Name	Age	Birthday	Accommodation	City/Town	Country
David	15	12th March	Small house	Paris	France
Marine	9	13th June	Small flat	Biarritz	France
Jean	14	9th January	Big flat	Nouméa	New Caledonia
Paul	12	20th August	Modern house	Berlin	Germany
Suzanne	13	1st September	Beautiful house	Dakar	Senegal

UNIT 4
Things I like/dislike:
school subjects & teachers

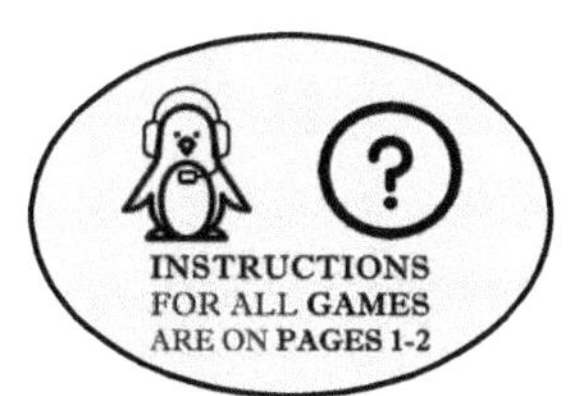

Quelles matières étudies-tu?						*What subjects do you study?*	
Quelle matière tu (n') aimes (pas)? Pourquoi?						*Which subject do you (**not**) like? Why?*	
Tu aimes le français? Pourquoi?						*Do you like French? Why?*	

Au collège, j'étudie *At school, I study*			l'allemand / l'histoire / les sciences / etc.				
J'aime *I like*	**l'**	allemand *German* anglais *English* espagnol *Spanish* histoire *history*	**car** *because* **mais** *but*	**c'est** *it is* **ce n'est pas** *it is not*	amusant *fun* compliqué *complicated* ennuyeux *boring* facile *easy* fatigant *tiring* intéressant *interesting* utile *useful*		
Je n'aime pas *I don't like*	**le**	dessin *art* français *French*					
Mon ami(e) aime *My friend likes*	**l'**	éducation civique *citizenship* éducation physique *PE* informatique *ICT*					
Mon ami(e) n'aime pas *My friend does not like*	**la**	chimie *chemistry* géographie *geography*					
	les	langues *languages* mathématiques *maths* sciences *science*					

De plus,	j'adore ça *I love it* j'aime ça *I like it*	**parce que** *because*	j'apprends beaucoup — *I learn a lot* c'est utile pour le futur — *it is useful for the future* j'ai des amis en classe — *I have friends in class*		
			le professeur est *the teacher (m) is* **la professeure est** *the teacher (f) is*	**assez** *quite* **très** *very*	amusant(e) *funny* bon(ne) *good* ennuyeux/euse *boring* méchant(e) *mean* patient(e) *patient* sympathique *nice*

UNIT 4 – FIND SOMEONE WHO – Student Cards

J'aime l'allemand. Je n'aime pas le dessin. **CHARLES**	J'aime les mathématiques. Je n'aime pas l'histoire. **ANTHONY**	J'adore le français. Je n'aime pas l'éducation physique. **LAURE**	J'aime le dessin et j'adore les langues. **MARTINE**
J'aime l'espagnol. Je n'aime pas l'histoire. **MICHEL**	J'aime l'informatique. Je n'aime pas la chimie. **JEAN**	J'aime l'anglais. Je n'aime pas le dessin. **MARIE**	J'aime les mathématiques. Je n'aime pas la chimie. **GEORGES**
J'aime l'anglais et j'aime aussi l'informatique. **JOËL**	J'aime l'informatique. Je n'aime pas les sciences. **HÉLÈNE**	J'aime les sciences. Je n'aime pas l'histoire. **JULIE**	J'aime l'histoire. Je n'aime pas les sciences. **LUCIE**
J'aime la chimie. Je n'aime pas l'allemand. **FERNAND**	J'adore le français. Je n'aime pas les sciences. **CARLA**	J'adore les langues. Je n'aime pas le dessin. **AURORE**	J'aime la géographie. Je n'aime pas l'anglais. **ALBANE**

UNIT 4 – FIND SOMEONE WHO – Student Grid

	Find someone who...	Name
1.	...likes maths.	
2.	...likes Spanish.	
3.	...likes German.	
4.	...likes history.	
5.	...likes geography.	
6.	...doesn't like German.	
7.	...loves languages.	
8.	...likes English.	
9.	...likes chemistry.	
10.	...doesn't like PE.	
11.	...likes ICT.	
12.	...loves French.	
13.	...doesn't like history.	

UNIT 4 – ORAL PING PONG – Person A

ENGLISH 1	FRENCH 1	ENGLISH 2	FRENCH 2
I don't like German because it is boring.	Je n'aime pas l'allemand car c'est ennuyeux.	**I don't like PE because it is tiring.**	Je n'aime pas l'éducation physique car c'est fatigant.
I like French because it is fun.		**I don't like PE because it is boring.**	
My friend likes geography because it is interesting.	Mon ami aime la géographie car c'est intéressant.	**I like chemistry because it is fun and interesting.**	J'aime la chimie car c'est amusant et intéressant.
I like chemistry because it is fun.		**I don't like maths because it is boring and complicated.**	
I like ICT because it is useful.	J'aime l'informatique car c'est utile.	**I like science but it is complicated.**	J'aime les sciences mais c'est compliqué.
My friend doesn't like art because it is boring.		**I like PE but it is tiring.**	
My friend doesn't like history because it is boring.	Mon ami n'aime pas l'histoire car c'est ennuyeux.	**My friend likes French but it is complicated.**	Mon ami aime le français mais c'est compliqué.
I like history because it is interesting.		**I like ICT because the teacher is good.**	
I don't like chemistry because it is complicated.	Je n'aime pas la chimie parce que c'est compliqué.	**I like English because I have friends in class.**	J'aime l'anglais parce que j'ai des amis en classe.
I like Spanish because it is fun.		**I like German but it isn't easy.**	

UNIT 4 – ORAL PING PONG – Person B

ENGLISH 1	FRENCH 1	ENGLISH 2	FRENCH 2
I don't like German because it is boring.		I don't like PE because it is tiring.	
I like French because it is fun.	J'aime le français car c'est amusant.	I don't like PE because it is boring.	Je n'aime pas l'éducation physique car c'est ennuyeux.
My friend likes geography because it is interesting.		I like chemistry because it is fun and interesting.	
I like chemistry because it is fun.	J'aime la chimie parce que c'est amusant.	I don't like maths because it is boring and complicated.	Je n'aime pas les mathématiques car c'est ennuyeux et compliqué.
I like ICT because it is useful.		I like science but it is complicated.	
My friend doesn't like art because it is boring.	Mon ami n'aime pas le dessin car c'est ennuyeux.	I like PE but it is tiring.	J'aime l'éducation physique mais c'est fatigant.
My friend doesn't like history because it is boring.		My friend likes French but it is complicated.	
I like history because it is interesting.	J'aime l'histoire car c'est intéressant.	I like ICT because the teacher is good.	J'aime l'informatique car le professeur est bon.
I don't like chemistry because it is complicated.		I like English because it is useful.	
I like Spanish because it is fun.	J'aime l'espagnol parce que c'est amusant.	I like German but it isn't easy.	J'aime l'allemand mais ce n'est pas facile.

No Snakes No Ladders

START	1 I don't like German.	2 I like geography.	3 What subjects do you study?	4 Do you like French?	5 I like art and history.	6 Do you like science?	7 I like ICT and Spanish.
15 I study science, maths and English.	14 I like languages because they are useful.	13 At school I study German and French.	12 I like ICT because it is useful and I have friends in class.	11 I don't like science because it is boring.	10 I like art because the teacher (F) is good.	9 I like French because it is fun and the teacher is good.	8 I don't like chemistry because it is complicated.
16 My friend likes Spanish because he learns a lot.	17 My friend (F) likes maths.	18 I like PE but my friend (M) likes music because it is fun.	19 My friend (F) likes history because it is interesting.	20 I don't like Spanish because it is complicated.	21 I like maths because it is fun and useful and the teacher (F) is good.	22 I don't like maths because it is complicated.	23 Do you like music?
FINISH	30 I like maths because it is useful but it is complicated.	29 I like PE because I have friends in class but it is very tiring.	28 My brother likes science because it is useful for the future.	27 I like science because it is fun and interesting.	26 Why do you like PE?	25 What subjects do you study? Why?	24 Do you like French? Why?

No Snakes No Ladders

DÉPART	1 Je n'aime pas l'allemand.	2 J'aime la géographie.	3 Quelles matières étudies-tu?	4 Tu aimes le français?	5 J'aime le dessin et l'histoire.	6 Tu aimes les sciences?
15 J'étudie les sciences, les maths et l'anglais.	14 J'aime les langues car c'est utile.	13 Au collège j'étudie l'allemand et le français.	12 J'aime l'informatique car c'est utile et j'ai des amis en classe.	11 Je n'aime pas les sciences car c'est ennuyeux.	10 J'aime le dessin car la professeure est bonne.	9 J'aime le français car c'est amusant et le professeur est bon.
16 Mon ami aime l'espagnol car il apprend beaucoup.	17 Mon amie aime les maths.	18 J'aime l'éducation physique mais mon ami aime la musique car c'est amusant.	19 Mon amie aime l'histoire car c'est intéressant.	20 Je n'aime pas l'espagnol car c'est compliqué.	21 J'aime les maths car c'est amusant et utile et la professeure est bonne.	22 Je n'aime pas les maths car c'est compliqué.
ARRIVÉE	30 J'aime les maths car c'est utile, mais c'est compliqué.	29 J'aime l'éducation physique car j'ai des amis en classe, mais c'est très fatigant.	28 Mon frère aime les sciences car c'est utile pour le futur.	27 J'aime les sciences car c'est amusant et intéressant.	26 Pourquoi aimes-tu l'éducation physique?	25 Quelles matières étudies-tu? Pourquoi

7	J'aime l'informatique et l'espagnol.
8	Je n'aime pas la chimie car c'est compliqué.
23	Tu aimes la musique?
24	Tu aimes le français? Pourquoi?

UNIT 4 – STAIRCASE TRANSLATION

Hi. My name is Anna. I am from Paris, but I live in Cannes.

Hi. My name is Anna. I am from Paris, but I live in Cannes. I go to the 'Collège Victor Hugo'.

Hi. My name is Anna. I am from Paris, but I live in Cannes. I go to the 'Collège Victor Hugo'. I study English, maths, science, art, history, geography, PE, technology and French.

Hi. My name is Anna. I am from Paris, but I live in Cannes. I go to the 'Collège Victor Hugo'. I study English, maths, science, art, history, geography, PE, technology and French. I like languages because they are fun and useful for the future and the teacher is good.

Hi. My name is Anna. I am from Paris, but I live in Cannes. I go to the 'Collège Victor Hugo'. I study English, maths, science, art, history, geography, PE, technology and French. I like languages because they are fun and useful for the future and the teacher is good. I don't like science...

* Hi. My name is Anna. I am from Paris, but I live in Cannes. I go to the 'Collège Victor Hugo'. I study English, maths, science, art, history, geography, PE, technology and French. I like languages because they are fun and useful for the future and the teacher is good. I don't like science and maths because it's boring and complicated.

* Translate the last step here:

 UNIT 4 – FASTER! 

Say:

1. I study English and French.
2. I like French because it is fun.
3. I like English because it is useful.
4. I like history because it is interesting.
5. I don't like science because it is complicated.
6. I don't like maths.
7. My friend Pierre likes art.
8. He likes art because it is easy.
9. He doesn't like history because it is boring.
10. What subjects do you like? Why?

	Time	Mistakes	Referee's name
1			
2			
3			
4			

UNIT 4 – THINGS IN COMMON

	1	2	3	4	5
Comment tu t'appelles?					
Quel âge as-tu?					
Quel est le mois de ton anniversaire?					
Tu habites dans une maison ou un appartement?					
Tu préfères le français ou les mathématiques?					
Tu préfères la géographie ou l'histoire?					
Tu préfères l'informatique ou l'anglais?					
Tu préfères l'éducation physique ou le dessin?					
Quelle est ta matière préférée?					

UNIT 4 – COMMUNICATIVE DRILLS

1	2	3
What subjects do you like? - I like maths because it is interesting and useful. I also like science because it is fun. **What subjects do you not like?** - I don't like history because it is boring.	**What subjects do you like?** - I like Spanish because it is interesting and useful. I also like English because it is fun. **What subjects do you not like?** - I don't like science because it is tiring and boring.	**What subjects do you like?** - I like history because it is interesting and fun. I also like science because it is useful. **What subjects do you not like?** - I don't like PE because it is tiring.
4	5	6
What subjects do you like? - I like ICT because it is interesting and useful and I have friends in class. **What subjects do you not like?** - I don't like history because it is boring and complicated.	**What subjects do you like?** - I like chemistry because it is interesting but complicated. I also like Spanish because I have friends in class and I learn a lot. **What subjects do you not like?** - I don't like maths because it is boring.	**What subjects do you like?** - I like art because it is easy and fun and the teacher is good. **What subjects do you not like?** - I don't like ICT because it is boring and the teacher is mean.
7	8	9
What subjects do you like? - I like French because it is interesting and fun. I also like science because I learn a lot. **What subjects do you not like?** - I don't like citizenship because it isn't useful for the future.	**What subjects do you like?** - I like maths because it is interesting and fun and I learn a lot in class. **What subjects do you not like?** - I don't like PE because it is tiring and not very useful.	**What subjects do you like?** - I like geography because it is interesting and useful. I also like science because the teacher is good. **What subjects do you not like?** - I don't like art because it is boring and complicated.

UNIT 4 – COMMUNICATIVE DRILLS REFEREE CARD

1	2	3
Quelles matières tu aimes? - J'aime les mathématiques car c'est intéressant et utile. J'aime aussi les sciences car c'est amusant. **Quelles matières tu n'aimes pas?** - Je n'aime pas l'histoire car c'est ennuyeux.	**Quelles matières tu aimes?** - J'aime l'espagnol car c'est intéressant et utile. J'aime aussi l'anglais car c'est amusant. **Quelles matières tu n'aimes pas?** - Je n'aime pas les sciences car c'est fatigant et ennuyeux.	**Quelles matières tu aimes?** - J'aime l'histoire car c'est intéressant et amusant. J'aime aussi les sciences car c'est utile. **Quelles matières tu n'aimes pas?** - Je n'aime pas l'éducation physique car c'est fatigant.
4	**5**	**6**
Quelles matières tu aimes? - J'aime l'informatique car c'est intéressant et utile et j'ai des amis en classe. **Quelles matières tu n'aimes pas?** - Je n'aime pas l'histoire car c'est ennuyeux et compliqué.	**Quelles matières tu aimes?** - J'aime la chimie car c'est intéressant mais compliqué. J'aime aussi l'espagnol car j'ai des amis en classe et j'apprends beaucoup. **Quelles matières tu n'aimes pas?** - Je n'aime pas les mathématiques car c'est ennuyeux.	**Quelles matières tu aimes?** - J'aime le dessin car c'est facile et amusant et le professeur est bon. **Quelles matières tu n'aimes pas?** - Je n'aime pas l'informatique car c'est ennuyeux et le professeur est méchant.
7	**8**	**9**
Quelles matières tu aimes? - J'aime le francais car c'est intéressant et amusant. J'aime aussi les sciences car j'apprends beaucoup. **Quelles matières tu n'aimes pas?** - Je n'aime pas l'éducation civique car ce n'est pas utile pour lc futur.	**Quelles matières tu aimes?** - J'aime les mathématiques car c'est intéressant et amusant et j'apprends beaucoup en classe. **Quelles matières tu n'aimes pas?** - Je n'aime pas l'éducation physique car c'est fatigant et pas très utile.	**Quelles matières tu aimes?** - J'aime la géographie car c'est intéressant et utile. J'aime aussi les sciences car le professeur est bon. **Quelles matières tu n'aimes pas?** - Je n'aime pas le dessin car c'est ennuyeux et compliqué.

UNIT 4 – SURVEY

	What is your name? **Comment tu t'appelles?**	How old are you? **Que âge as-tu?**	What is your school called? **Comment s'appelle ton collège?**	What subjects do you like? Why? **Quelles matières tu aimes? Pourquoi?**	What subjects do you **not** like? Why? **Quelles matières tu n'aimes pas? Pourquoi?**
e.g.	*Je m'appelle Sylvie.*	*J'ai douze ans.*	*Mon collège s'appelle Collège Beau Soleil.*	*J'aime les sciences parce que c'est utile.*	*Je n'aime pas l'histoire car c'est ennuyeux.*
1.					
2.					
3.					
4.					
5.					
6.					
7.					

UNIT 4 – ANSWERS

FIND SOMEONE WHO

	Find someone who...	Name
1.	...likes maths.	Anthony / Georges
2.	...likes Spanish.	Michel
3.	...likes German.	Charles
4.	...likes history.	Lucie
5.	...likes geography.	Albane
6.	...doesn't like German.	Fernand
7.	...loves languages.	Aurore / Martine
8.	...likes English.	Marie / Joël
9.	...likes chemistry.	Fernand
10.	...doesn't like PE.	Laure
11.	...likes ICT.	Hélène / Jean / Joël
12.	...loves French.	Carla
13.	...doesn't like history.	Julie

STAIRCASE TRANSLATION

Salut. Je m'appelle Anna. Je suis de Paris, mais j'habite à Cannes. Je vais au 'Collège Victor Hugo'. J'étudie l'anglais, les mathématiques, les sciences, le dessin, l'histoire, la géographie, l'éducation physique, la technologie et le français. J'aime les langues car c'est amusant et utile pour le futur et le professeur est bon. Je n'aime pas les sciences et les mathématiques car c'est ennuyeux et compliqué.

FASTER!

REFEREE SOLUTION:

1. J'étudie l'anglais et le français.
2. J'aime le français parce que c'est amusant.
3. J'aime l'anglais parce que c'est utile.
4. J'aime l'histoire car c'est intéressant.
5. Je n'aime pas les sciences car c'est compliqué.
6. Je n'aime pas les mathématiques.
7. Mon ami Pierre aime le dessin.
8. Il aime le dessin car c'est facile.
9. Il n'aime pas l'histoire car c'est ennuyeux.
10. Quelles matières tu aimes? Pourquoi?

THINGS IN COMMON

Students give their own answers to the questions and make a note of which students they have things in common with.

UNIT 5
Things I like/dislike: free time

Qu'est-ce que tu aimes faire pendant ton temps libre?				*What do you like to do in your free time?*
Pendant mon temps libre *In my free time* **Quand j'ai du temps libre** *When I have free time*	**j'adore** *I love* **j'aime** *I like* **je déteste** *I hate*	**aller** *to go*	**à la pêche** — *fishing* **à la piscine** — *to the pool* **au centre commercial** *to the shopping mall* **au centre sportif** *to the sports centre* **au gymnase** — *to the gym* **au parc** — *to the park* **chez mon ami** *to my friend's house* **me promener** — *for a walk*	**avec ma sœur** *with my sister* **avec mes amis** *with my friends* **avec mes parents** *with my parents* **avec mon ami Pierre** *with my friend Pierre* **avec mon frère** *with my brother*
		faire *to do*	**de la natation** — *swimming* **de la randonnée** — *hiking* **de l'équitation** — *horse riding* **du footing** — *jogging* **du sport** — *sport* **du vélo** — *cycling*	
		jouer *to play*	**à la PlayStation** **au basket** — *basketball* **au foot** — *football* **au tennis** — *tennis* **aux cartes** — *cards* **aux échecs** — *chess* **aux jeux vidéo** — *videogames* **sur l'ordinateur** *on the computer*	

J'aime cela *I like it* **Je n'aime pas cela** *I don't like it*	**car/parce que** *because*	**c'est** *it is* **ce n'est pas** *it is not*	**amusant** — *fun* **ennuyeux** — *boring* **fatigant** — *tiring* **génial** — *great* **intéressant** — *interesting* **sain** — *healthy*

UNIT 5 – FIND SOMEONE WHO – Student Cards

Pendant mon temps libre, j'adore jouer à la Playstation. **VINCENT**	Pendant mon temps libre, j'aime faire de la randonnée. **PHILIPPE**	Pendant mon temps libre, j'aime faire de l'équitation. **PATRICIA**	Pendant mon temps libre, j'adore faire du vélo. **BÉATRICE**
Pendant mon temps libre, j'aime jouer aux jeux vidéo. **FRANCIS**	Pendant mon temps libre, j'aime jouer au basket. **ÉRIC**	Pendant mon temps libre, j'aime jouer aux échecs. **CATHERINE**	Pendant mon temps libre, j'aime aller au centre commercial. **ANDRÉA**
Pendant mon temps libre, j'adore aller au gymnase pour faire de la musculation. **JEAN-FRANCOIS**	Pendant mon temps libre, j'aime faire du footing au parc. **DANIELLE**	Pendant mon temps libre, j'aime aller à la piscine pour faire de la natation. **ÉMILIE**	Pendant mon temps libre, j'adore aller me promener au parc. **LÉA**
Pendant mon temps libre, j'adore aller à la pêche. **GUILLAUME**	Pendant mon temps libre, j'adore aller me promener au parc avec ma sœur. **DELPHINE**	Pendant mon temps libre, j'adore aller au centre sportif. **SOPHIE**	Pendant mon temps libre, j'aime aller chez mon amie. **CAROLINE**

UNIT 5 – FIND SOMEONE WHO – Student Grid

Find someone who...	Name(s)
Comment tu t'appelles? *What is your name?* **Qu'est-ce que tu aimes faire pendant ton temps libre?** *What do you like to do in your free time?*	
1. …loves playing PlayStation.	
2. …loves cycling.	
3. …likes going to the pool to do swimming.	
4. …likes going to the shopping centre.	
5. …loves going to the sports centre.	
6. …likes playing basketball.	
7. …likes playing videogames.	
8. …loves going for a walk in the park.	
9. …loves going fishing.	
10. …likes going to their friend's house.	
11. …likes playing chess.	
12. …likes hiking.	
13. …loves going to the gym to do weights.	
14. …loves to go jogging in the park.	
15. …likes to do horse riding.	

UNIT 5 – ORAL PING PONG – Person A

ENGLISH 1	FRENCH 1	ENGLISH 2	FRENCH 2
In my free time I love to do cycling.	Pendant mon temps libre, j'adore faire du vélo.	In my free time I love to do jogging.	Pendant mon temps libre, j'adore faire du footing.
In my free time I love playing cards.		In my free time I love playing basketball.	
When I have free time I hate to do sport.	Quand j'ai du temps libre, je déteste faire du sport.	When I have free time I hate to do horse riding.	Quand j'ai du temps libre, je déteste faire de l'équitation.
When I have free time I hate to go to the swimming pool.		When I have free time I hate to go to shopping centre.	
In my free time I like to do horse riding.	Pendant mon temps libre, j'aime faire de l'équitation.	In my free time I like to go fishing.	Pendant mon temps libre, j'aime aller à la pêche.
In my free time I like to do jogging.		In my free time I like to do swimming.	
In my free time I like to go to the sports centre.	Pendant mon temps libre, j'aime aller au centre sportif.	In my free time I like to go to the park.	Pendant mon temps libre, j'aime aller au parc.
In my free time I like to go to the gym.		In my free time I like to play cards.	
When I have free time I like to go to my friend's house.	Quand j'ai du temps libre, j'aime aller chez mon ami.	When I have free time I like to play chess with my brother.	Quand j'ai du temps libre, j'aime jouer aux échecs avec mon frère.
When I have free time I like to go for a walk with my friends.		When I have free time I like to play video games with my sister.	

UNIT 5 – ORAL PING PONG – Person B

ENGLISH 1	FRENCH 1	ENGLISH 2	FRENCH 2
In my free time I love to do cycling.		In my free time I love to do jogging.	
In my free time I love playing cards.	Pendant mon temps libre, j'adore jouer aux cartes.	In my free time I love playing basketball.	Pendant mon temps libre, j'adore jouer au basket.
When I have free time I hate to do sport.		When I have free time I hate to do horse riding.	
When I have free time I hate to go to the swimming pool.	Quand j'ai du temps libre, je déteste aller à la piscine.	When I have free time I hate to go to shopping centre.	Quand j'ai du temps libre, je déteste aller au centre commercial.
In my free time I like to do horse riding.		In my free time I like to go fishing.	
In my free time I like to do jogging.	Pendant mon temps libre, j'aime faire du footing.	In my free time I like to do swimming.	Pendant mon temps libre, j'aime faire de la natation.
In my free time I like to go to the sports centre.		In my free time I like to go to the park.	
In my free time I like to go to the gym.	Pendant mon temps libre, j'aime aller au gymnase.	In my free time I like to play cards.	Pendant mon temps libre, j'aime jouer aux cartes.
When I have free time I like to go to my friend's house.		When I have free time I like to play chess with my brother.	
When I have free time I like to go for a walk with my friends.	Quand j'ai du temps libre, j'aime aller me promener avec mes amis.	When I have free time I like to play video games with my sister.	Quand j'ai du temps libre, j'aime jouer aux jeux vidéo avec ma sœur.

No Snakes No Ladders

START

1 — When I have free time I like to go to my friend's (M) house.

2 — In my free time I hate to go swimming because it is tiring.

3 — In my free time I like to play tennis because it is fun.

4 — In my free time I like to play cards because it is fun.

5 — When I have free time I like to play videogames.

6 — What do you like to do in your free time?

7 — When I have free time I like to DO jogging.

8 — In my free time I like to play basketball and to DO swimming.

9 — When I have free time I love to go to the gym.

10 — What do you like to do in your free time?

11 — When I have free time I like to go for a walk.

12 — What do you like to do in your free time?

13 — In my free time I like to go fishing.

14 — In my free time I like to go to the shopping centre.

15 — When I have free time.

16 — In my free time.

17 — When I have free time I like to go hiking but it is tiring.

18 — When I have free time I like to go for a walk with my friends.

19 — In my free time I like to go to the park with my brother.

20 — When I have free time I like to play PlayStation with my friend.

21 — In my free time I like to DO jogging with my friends.

22 — When I have free time I hate to the shopping mall because it is boring

23 — When I have free time I hate to go horse riding because it is boring.

24 — In my free time I like to play tennis with my sister.

25 — In my free time I like to go to my friend's house.

26 — What do you like to do in your free time?

27 — In my free time I like to play football with my brother and my friends.

28 — What do you like to do in your free time?

29 — In my free time I like to play basketball with my friends.

30 — When I have free time I like to DO cycling with my brother.

FINISH

No Snakes No Ladders

DÉPART	**1** Quand j'ai du temps libre, j'aime aller chez mon ami.	**2** Pendant mon temps libre, je déteste faire de la natation car c'est fatigant.	**3** Pendant mon temps libre, j'aime jouer au tennis car c'est amusant.	**4** Pendant mon temps libre, j'aime jouer au cartes car c'est amusant.	**5** Quand j'ai du temps libre, j'aime jouer aux jeux vidéo.	**6** Qu'est-ce que tu aimes faire pendant ton temps libre?	**7** Quand j'ai du temps libre, j'aime faire du footing.
15 Quand j'ai du temps libre.	**14** Pendant mon temps libre, j'aime aller au centre commercial.	**13** Pendant mon temps libre, j'aime aller à la pêche.	**12** Qu'est-ce que tu aimes faire pendant ton temps libre?	**11** Quand j'ai du temps libre j'aime aller me promener.	**10** Qu'est-ce que tu aimes faire pendant ton temps libre?	**9** Quand j'ai du temps libre, j'adore aller au gymnase.	**8** Pendant mon temps libre, j'aime jouer au basket et faire de la natation.
16 Pendant mon temps libre.	**17** Quand j'ai du temps libre, j'aime faire de la randonnée mais c'est fatigant.	**18** Quand j'ai du temps libre, j'aime aller me promener avec mes amis.	**19** Quand j'ai du temps libre, j'aime aller au parc avec mon frère.	**20** Quand j'ai du temps libre, j'aime jouer à la Playstation avec mon ami.	**21** Pendant mon temps libre, j'aime faire du footing avec mes amis.	**22** Quand j'ai du temps libre, je déteste aller au centre commercial car c'est ennuyeux.	**23** Quand j'ai du temps libre, je déteste faire de l'équitation car c'est ennuyeux.
ARRIVÉE	**30** Quand j'ai du temps libre, j'aime faire du vélo avec mon frère.	**29** Pendant mon temps libre, j'aime jouer au basket avec mes amis.	**28** Qu'est-ce que tu aimes faire pendant ton temps libre?	**27** Pendant mon temps libre, j'aime jouer au foot avec mon frère et mes amis.	**26** Qu'est-ce que tu aimes faire pendant ton temps libre?	**25** Pendant mon temps libre, j'aime aller chez mon ami.	**24** Pendant mon temps libre, j'aime jouer au tennis avec ma sœur.

UNIT 5 – STAIRCASE TRANSLATION

In my free time.

In my free time I like to play tennis.

In my free time I like to play tennis and basketball with my friends.

In my free time I like to play tennis and basketball with my friends. I also like to play video games and PlayStation…

In my free time I like to play tennis and basketball with my friends because it is fun and exciting. I also like to play video games and PlayStation with my friends because it is fun.

* In my free time I like to play tennis and basketball with my friends. I also like to play video games and PlayStation with my friends because it is fun. However, *(cependant)* I don't like to go fishing because it is boring.

* Translate the
last step here:

 UNIT 5 – FASTER! 

Say:

1. What do you like to do in your free time?
2. I like to play video games because it is fun.
3. I also like to do sport because it is fun and healthy.
4. I love to go cycling because it is great.
5. I also love to go to the gym because it is fun and healthy.
6. I don't like to go horse riding because it is boring.
7. I hate to go jogging because it is tiring.
8. I don't like to go hiking because it is boring and tiring.

	Time	Mistakes	Referee's name
1			
2			
3			
4			

UNIT 5 – FAST & FURIOUS – Version 1

1. J'adore _________ du vélo avec mes amis.
2. J'aime ________ aux échecs avec mon frère.
3. Je déteste _______ au centre sportif.
4. J'adore _______ du sport.
5. J'adore _______ chez mon ami.
6. J'aime _______ de la randonnée.
7. J'aime beaucoup _______ aux jeux vidéo.
8. J'adore _______ de la natation.
9. J'aime _______ au parc.
10. J'aime beaucoup _______ aux cartes.

	Time 1	Time 2	Time 3	Time 4
Time				
Mistakes				

UNIT 5 – FAST & FURIOUS – Version 2

1. J'adore _________ de la natation avec mon ami.
2. J'aime ________ au tennis avec ma sœur.
3. Je déteste _______ au centre commercial.
4. J'adore _______ de l'équitation.
5. J'aime beaucoup _______ chez ma meilleure amie.
6. J'adore _______ du footing au parc.
7. J'aime beaucoup _______ au foot.
8. J'adore _______ à la plage.
9. J'aime beaucoup _______ aux échecs.
10. J'aime _______ me promener au parc avec mon chien.

	Time 1	Time 2	Time 3	Time 4
Time				
Mistakes				

UNIT 5 – COMMUNICATIVE DRILLS

1	2	3
What do you like doing in your free time? - I like to go to my friend's house and play PlayStation with him. It's a lot of fun. And you? **In my free time I like to go to the shopping centre or to play football with my friends.**	**What do you like doing in your free time?** - I like to go to my friend's house and play cards or chess with her. It's a lot of fun. And you? **In my free time I like to go to the swimming pool with my brother and sister. I like to swim because it is healthy.**	**What do you <u>not</u> like doing in your free time?** - I don't like to go hiking with my parents. It is tiring and very boring. And you? What do you not like doing in your free time? **I don't like to go fishing with my dad. I don't like it because it is very boring.**
4	5	6
What do you like doing in your free time? - In my free time I like to do sport because it is healthy and fun. And you? **In my free time I like to go to the pool.**	**What do you like doing in your free time?** - I like to go to my friend's house and play chess and video games with him. It's fun. And you? **In my free time I like to go to the sports centre or to the park with my friends.**	**What do you like doing in your free time?** - I like to play on the computer, go horse riding and fishing. It's great. And you? **In my free time I like to go to the gym and to go jogging. It is tiring but fun.**
7	8	9
Do you like to go swimming at the pool? - No, I don't like it because it is tiring and boring. **Do you like to play football and basketball?** - Yes I like it a lot. It's a lot of fun.	**Do you like to go to the shopping centre?** - No, I don't like it because it is boring. **Do you like to play video games.** - Yes I like it because it's great.	**Do you like to go to the gym?** - No, I don't like it because it is very tiring and boring. **Do you like to play chess?** - Yes I like it a lot because it's interesting. **Do you like to play cards?** - Yes, I love it. It is very fun.

UNIT 5 – COMMUNICATIVE DRILLS
REFEREE CARD

1	2	3
Qu'est-ce que tu aimes faire pendant ton temps libre? - J'aime aller chez mon ami et jouer à la Playstation avec lui. C'est très amusant. Et toi? **Pendant mon temps libre, j'aime aller au centre commercial ou jouer au foot avec mes amis.**	**Qu'est-ce que tu aimes faire pendant ton temps libre?** - J'aime aller chez mon amie et jouer aux cartes ou aux échecs avec elle. C'est très amusant. Et toi? **Pendant mon temps libre, j'aime aller à la piscine avec mon frère et ma sœur. J'aime nager car c'est sain.**	**Qu'est-ce que tu n'aimes pas faire pendant ton temps libre?** - Je n'aime pas faire de la randonnée avec mes parents. C'est fatigant et très ennuyeux. Et toi? Qu'est-ce que tu n'aimes pas faire pendant ton temps libre? **Je n'aime pas aller à la pêche avec mon père. Je n'aime pas cela car c'est très ennuyeux.**
4	**5**	**6**
Qu'est-ce que tu aimes faire pendant ton temps libre? - Pendant mon temps libre j'aime faire du sport car c'est sain et amusant. Et toi? **Pendant mon temps libre, j'aime aller à la piscine.**	**Qu'est-ce que tu aimes faire pendant ton temps libre?** - J'aime aller chez mon ami et jouer aux échecs et aux jeux vidéo avec lui. C'est amusant. Et toi? **Pendant mon temps libre, j'aime aller au centre sportif ou au parc avec mes amis.**	**Qu'est-ce que tu aimes faire pendant ton temps libre?** - J'aime jouer sur l'ordinateur, faire de l'équitation et aller à la pêche. C'est génial. Et toi? **Pendant mon temps libre, j'aime aller au gymnase et faire du footing. C'est fatigant mais amusant.**
7	**8**	**9**
Tu aimes faire de la natation à la piscine? - Non, je n'aime pas cela car c'est fatigant et ennuyeux. **Tu aimes jouer au foot et au basket?** - Oui, j'aime beaucoup cela. C'est très amusant.	**Tu aimes aller au centre commercial?** - Non, je n'aime pas cela car c'est ennuyeux. **Tu aimes jouer aux jeux vidéo?** - Oui, j'aime cela car c'est génial.	**Tu aimes aller au gymnase?** - Non, je n'aime pas cela car c'est très fatigant et ennuyeux. **Tu aimes jouer aux échecs?** - Oui, j'aime beaucoup cela parce que c'est intéressant. **Tu aimes jouer aux cartes?** - Oui, j'adore cela. C'est très amusant.

UNIT 5 – SURVEY

	What is your name?	Where do you live?	What school subjects do you like? Why?	What do you like to do in your free time? Why?	What do you not like to do in your free time? Why not?
	Comment tu t'appelles?	Où habites-tu?	Quelles matières tu aimes? Pourquoi?	Qu'est-ce que tu aimes faire pendant ton temps libre? Pourquoi?	Qu'est-ce que tu n'aimes pas faire pendant ton temps libre? Pourquoi?
e.g.	*Je m'appelle Jean.*	*J'habite à Paris mais je suis de Rennes.*	*J'aime les sciences parce que c'est intéressant.*	*J'aime faire du sport parce que c'est amusant.*	*Je n'aime pas jouer aux échecs parce que c'est ennuyeux.*
1.					
2.					
3.					
4.					
5.					
6.					
7.					

UNIT 5 – ANSWERS

FIND SOMEONE WHO

	Find someone who...	Name
1.	...loves playing PlayStation.	Vincent
2.	...loves cycling.	Béatrice
3.	...likes going to the pool to do swimming.	Émilie
4.	...likes going to the shopping centre.	Andréa
5.	...loves going to the sports centre.	Sophie
6.	...likes playing basketball.	Éric
7.	...likes playing videogames.	Francis
8.	...loves going for a walk in the park.	Léa / Delphine
9.	...loves going fishing.	Guillaume
10.	...likes going to their friend's house.	Caroline
11.	...likes playing chess.	Catherine
12.	...likes hiking.	Philippe
13.	...loves going to the gym to do bodybuilding.	Jean-François
14.	...loves to go jogging in the park.	Danielle
15.	...likes to do horse riding.	Patricia

STAIRCASE TRANSLATION

Pendant mon temps libre, j'aime jouer au tennis et au basket avec mes amis. J'aime aussi jouer aux jeux vidéo et à la Playstation avec mes amis parce que c'est amusant. Cependant, je n'aime pas aller à la pêche parce que c'est ennuyeux.

FASTER! REFEREE SOLUTION:

1. Qu'est-ce que tu aimes faire pendant ton temps libre?
2. J'aime jouer aux jeux vidéo parce que c'est amusant.
3. J'aime aussi faire du sport parce que c'est amusant et sain.
4. J'adore faire du vélo parce que c'est génial.
5. J'adore aussi aller au gymnase parce que c'est amusant et sain.
6. Je n'aime pas faire de l'équitation parce que c'est ennuyeux.
7. Je déteste faire du footing parce que c'est fatigant.
8. Je n'aime pas faire de la randonnée parce que c'est ennuyeux et fatigant.

FAST & FURIOUS

VERSION 1

1. J'adore **faire** du vélo avec mes amis.
2. J'aime **jouer** aux échecs avec mon frère.
3. Je déteste **aller** au centre sportif.
4. J'adore **faire** du sport.
5. J'adore **aller** chez mon ami.
6. J'aime **faire** de la randonnée.
7. J'aime beaucoup **jouer** aux jeux vidéo.
8. J'adore **faire** de la natation.
9. J'aime **aller** au parc.
10. J'aime beaucoup **jouer** aux cartes.

VERSION 2

1. J'adore **faire** de la natation avec mon ami.
2. J'aime **jouer** au tennis avec ma sœur.
3. Je déteste **aller** au centre commercial.
4. J'adore **faire** de l'équitation.
5. J'aime beaucoup **aller** chez ma meilleure amie.
6. J'adore **faire** du footing au parc.
7. J'aime beaucoup **jouer** au foot.
8. J'adore **aller** à la plage.
9. J'aime beaucoup **jouer** aux échecs.
10. J'aime **aller** me promener au parc avec mon chien.

UNIT 6
Talking about my family members, saying their age, how well I get on with them. Counting to 100.

Combien de personnes il y a dans ta famille? Avec qui tu t'entends bien dans ta famille? Tu t'entends mal avec quelqu'un?		*How many people are there in your family?* *Who do you get on well with in your family?* *Do you get on badly with anyone?*		
	mon cousin, Tanguy. *my cousin, Tanguy.*		**un** *1*	**an**
Dans ma famille, j'ai *In my family, I have…*	**mon grand-père, Léon.** *my grandfather Léon.*		**deux** **trois** **quatre** **cinq** **six** **sept** **huit** **neuf** **dix**	
	mon père, Jean. *my father Jean.*	**Il a**		
	mon oncle, Yvan. *my uncle Yvan.*			
Il y a <u>quatre</u> personnes dans ma famille *There are <u>four</u> people in my family…*	**mon frère aîné, Ronan.** *my older brother Ronan.*		**onze** *11* **douze** *12* **treize** *13* **quatorze** *14* **quinze** *15*	
	mon frère cadet, Olivier. *my younger brother Olivier.*		**seize** *16*	
Je m'entends bien avec… *I get on well with…*	**ma cousine, Claire.** *my (girl) cousin Claire.*		**dix-sept** *17* **dix-huit** *18* **dix-neuf** *19* **vingt** *20*	
	ma grand-mère, Adeline. *my grandmother Adeline.*		**vingt-et-un** 21 **vingt-deux** 22 **trente** *30*	
	ma mère, Anne. *my mother Anne.*	**Elle a**	**trente-et-un** *31* **trente-deux** *32*	**ans**
Je ne m'entends pas bien avec… *I don't get on well with…*	**ma tante, Gisèle.** *my aunt Gisèle.*		**quarante** *40* **cinquante** *50* **soixante** *60* **soixante-dix** *70*	
	ma sœur aînée, Léa. *my older sister Léa.*		**quatre-vingts** *80* **quatre-vingt-dix** *90*	
	ma sœur cadette, Sophie. *my younger sister Sophie.*		**cent** *100*	

UNIT 6 – FIND SOMEONE WHO – Student Cards

Mon père a quarante-trois ans. **HUGO**	Mon père a cinquante-quatre ans. **DAVID**	Mon père a vingt-neuf ans. **ALICE**	Mon père a trente-huit ans. **ANTOINETTE**
Mon père a soixante-dix ans. **NATHAN**	Mon père a trente-quatre ans. **SONIA**	Mon père a vingt-six ans. **DANIEL**	Mon père a quarante-deux ans. **AMÉLIE**
Mon père a soixante ans. **MÉLANIE**	Mon père a quarante-neuf ans. **CLAIRE**	Mon père a quarante-huit ans. **FERNAND**	Mon père a cinquante-huit ans. **CHARLES**
Mon père a cinquante-huit ans. **ANNA**	Mon père a trente-sept ans. **CAROLINE**	Mon père a cinquante-et-un an. **BÉATRICE**	Mon père a soixante-dix ans. **JEANNE**

UNIT 6 – FIND SOMEONE WHO – Student Grid

Find someone whose father...		Name
Comment tu t'appelles *What is your name?* **Quel âge a ton père?** *How old is your father?*		
1.	...is 43 years old.	
2.	...is 54 years old.	
3.	...is 29 years old.	
4.	...is 38 years old.	
5.	...is 70 years old.	
6.	...is 34 years old.	
7.	...is 26 years old.	
8.	...is 42 years old.	
9.	...is 60 years old.	
10.	...is 49 years old.	
11.	...is 48 years old.	
12.	...is 58 years old.	
13.	...is 37 years old.	
14.	...is 51 years old.	

UNIT 6 – ORAL PING PONG – Person A

ENGLISH 1	FRENCH 1	ENGLISH 2	FRENCH 2
In my family there are four people.	Dans ma famille, il y a quatre personnes.	**My older brother is 14.**	Mon frère a quatorze ans.
My older sister is 15.		**I get on well with my brother.**	
My uncle is 52.	Mon oncle a cinquante-deux ans.	**My older sister is 18.**	Ma sœur aînée a dix-huit ans.
I get on well with my aunt.		**My uncle is 42.**	
My aunt is 38.	Ma tante a trente-huit ans.	**My cousin is 17.**	Mon cousin a dix-sept ans.
My cousin is 18.		**In my family there are five people.**	
My grandfather is 67.	Mon grand-père a soixante-sept ans.	**My mother is 40.**	Ma mère a quarante ans.
My mother is 36.		**My aunt is 45.**	
My grandmother is 65.	Ma grand-mère a soixante-cinq ans.	**My older brother is 15.**	Mon frère aîné a quinze ans.
My younger brother is 11.		**My grandfather is 80.**	

UNIT 6 – ORAL PING PONG – Person B

ENGLISH 1	FRENCH 1	ENGLISH 2	FRENCH 2
In my family there are four people.		**My older brother is 14.**	
My older sister is 15.	Ma sœur aînée a quinze ans.	**I get on with my brother.**	Je m'entends bien avec mon frère.
My uncle is 52.		**My older sister is 18.**	
I get on with my aunt.	Je m'entends bien avec ma tante.	**My uncle is 42.**	Mon oncle a quarante-deux ans.
My aunt is 38.		**My cousin is 17.**	
My cousin is 18.	Mon cousin a dix-huit ans.	**In my family there are five people.**	Dans ma famille, il y a cinq personnes.
My grandfather is 67.		**My mother is 40.**	
My mother is 36.	Ma mère a trente-six ans.	**My aunt is 45.**	Ma tante a quarante-cinq ans.
My grandmother is 65.		**My older brother is 15.**	
My younger brother is 11.	Mon frère cadet a onze ans.	**My grandfather is 80.**	Mon grand-père a quatre-vingts ans.

No Snakes No Ladders

#	Text
1	START — How many people are there your family?
2	In my family there are six people.
3	In my family there are eight people.
4	There are five people in my family.
5	There are four people in my family.
6	Do you get on well with your father?
7	Do you get on well with your mother?
8	I don't get on well with my mother.
9	I get on well with my older brother.
10	I don't get on well with my sister.
11	I don't get on well with my uncle.
12	How old is your uncle?
13	How old is your father?
14	How old is your mother?
15	How old is your sister?
16	My sister is eighteen.
17	My mother is forty-one.
18	Mi father is fifty.
19	My grandfather is seventy-eight.
20	My younger brother is fifteen.
21	My older brother is twenty.
22	How old is your grandfather?
23	How old is your mother?
24	My mother is thirty-six.
25	I get on well with my mother. She is forty-five.
26	I get on well with my uncle. He is thirty-seven.
27	I get on well with my grandfather. He is seventy.
28	My older brother is fourteen.
29	My younger brother is ten.
30	FINISH — My grandmother is seventy-six.

No Snakes No Ladders

DÉPART

1. Combien de personnes il y a dans ta famille?
2. Dans ma famille, il y a six personnes.
3. Dans ma famille, il y a huit personnes.
4. Il y a cinq personnes dans ma famille.
5. Il y a quatre personnes dans ma famille.
6. Tu t'entends bien avec ton père?
7. Tu t'entends bien avec ta mère?
8. Je ne m'entends pas bien avec ma mère.
9. Je m'entends bien avec mon frère aîné.
10. Je ne m'entends pas bien avec ma sœur.
11. Je ne m'entends pas bien avec mon oncle.
12. Quel âge a ton oncle?
13. Quel âge a ton père?
14. Quel âge a ta mère?
15. Quel âge a ta sœur?
16. Ma sœur a dix-huit ans.
17. Ma mère a quarante-et-un ans.
18. Mon père a cinquante ans.
19. Mon grand-père a soixante-dix-huit ans.
20. Mon frère cadet a quinze ans.
21. Mon frère aîné a vingt ans.
22. Quel âge a ton grand-père?
23. Quel âge a ta mère?
24. Ma mère a trente-six ans.
25. Je m'entends bien avec ma mère. Elle a quarante-cinq ans.
26. Je m'entends bien avec mon oncle. Il a trente-sept ans.
27. Je m'entends bien avec mon grand-père. Il a soixante-dix ans.
28. Mon frère aîné a quatorze ans.
29. Mon frère cadet a dix ans.
30. Ma grand-mère a soixante-seize ans.

ARRIVÉE

UNIT 6 – STAIRCASE TRANSLATION

My name is Suzanne. I am 11. I am from Paris.

My name is Suzanne. I am 11.
I am from Paris. In my family there are four people…

My name is Suzanne. I am 11. I am from Paris. In my family there are four people: my father, my mother, my brother and me.

My name is Suzanne. I am 11. I am from Paris. In my family there are four people: my father, my mother, my brother and me. I get on well with my father but I don't get on well with my mother.

My name is Suzanne. I am 11. I am from Paris. In my family there are four people: my father, my mother, my brother and me. I get on well with my father but I don't get on well with my mother. My father is 40 and my mother is 35. My sister is 15.

* My name is Suzanne. I am 11. I am from Paris. In my family there are four people: my father, my mother, my brother and me. I get on well with my father but I don't get on well with my mother. My father is 40 and my mother is 35. My sister is 15. How many people are there in your family? How old is your father? How old is your mother?

* Translate the
last step here:

⏱ UNIT 6 – FASTER! 🚀

Say:

1. In my family there are four people.
2. My father, my mother, my brother Julien and my sister Anna.
3. My father is 39.
4. My mother is 43.
5. My grandfather is 71.
6. My grandfather is 64.
7. I don't get on well with my father.
8. I get on well with my mother.
9. How many people are there in your family?
10. Do you get on well with your mother?

	Time	Mistakes	Referee's name
1			
2			
3			
4			

UNIT 6 – TRAPDOOR

| Ma Mon | grand-mère
grand-père
sœur
frère
mère
père
cousine
cousin
tante
oncle | a | dix
quinze
vingt-six
trente
trente-six
quarante
cinquante
soixante-dix
quatre-vingts | ans. | Son anniversaire | est le | neuf
vingt
dix-huit
trente
seize
vinft-deux
trente-et-un
quinze | janvier.
février.
avril.
mars.
mai.
juin.
août.
septembre. |

1. My grandfather is 80. His birthday is on 18 August.
2. My female cousin is 15. Her birthday is on 15 January.
3. My brother is six. His birthday is on 22 June.
4. My mother is 36. Her birthday is on 9 February.
5. My grandmother is 70. Her birthday is on 16 April.
6. My father is 50. His birthday in on 30 September.
7. My sister is 26. His birthday is on 31 March.

	Time 1	Time 2	Time 3	Time 4
Time				
Mistakes				

UNIT 6 – COMMUNICATIVE DRILLS

1	2	3
How many people are there in your family? - In my family there are six people. My mother, father, older brother, younger brother and my sister. **How old are your father? And your mother?** - My father is 38 and my mother is 37.	**How many people are there in your family?** - In my family there are four people. My mother, my father, my sister and I. **How old are your father? And your mother?** - My father is 42 and my mother is 35.	**How many people are there in your family?** - In my family there are three people. My mother, my father and I. **How old are your father? And your mother?** - My father is 52 and my mother is 36.

4	5	6
How old is your father? - My father is 60. **How old is your mother?** - My mother is 52 **Do you get on well with your father?** - Yes, I get on with my father but I don't get on with my mother.	**How old is your grandfather?** - My grandfather is 70. **How old is your grandmother?** - My grandmother is 72. **Do you get on well with your grandfather?** - No. I don't get on well my grandfather, but I get on with my grandmother.	**How old is your uncle Josh?** - My uncle Josh is 63. **How old is your aunt Linda?** - My aunt Linda is 67. **Do you get on well with your uncle and your aunt?** - I get on well my aunt, but I don't get on with my uncle.

7	8	9
How many people are there in your family? - In my family there are six people. My mother, my father, my two sisters, my brother and I. **How old are your father? And your mother?** - My father is 48 and my mother is 34.	**How old is your father?** - My father is 64. **How old is your mother?** - My mother is 52. **Do you get on well with your parents?** - Yes and no. I get on well with my mother, but I don't get on well with my father.	**What is your name?** - My name is Charles. **Where are you from?** - I am from London but I live in Paris. **How many people are there in your family?** - We are four in my family: my father, my mother, my sister and I. **Do you get on well with your parents *(tes parents)*?** - I get on with my father, but I don't get on with my mother.

UNIT 6 – COMMUNICATIVE DRILLS
REFEREE CARD

1	2	3
Combien de personnes il y a dans ta famille? - Dans ma famille, il y a six personnes. Ma mère, mon père, mon frère aîné, mon frère cadet et ma sœur. **Quel âge a ton père? Et ta mère?** - Mon père a trente-huit ans et ma mère a trente-sept ans.	**Combien de personnes il y a dans ta famille?** - Dans ma famille, il y a quatre personnes. Ma mère, mon père, ma sœur et moi. **Quel âge a ton père? Et ta mère?** - Mon père a quarante-deux ans et ma mère a trente-cinq ans.	**Combien de personnes il y a dans ta famille?** - Dans ma famille, il y a trois personnes. Ma mère, mon père et moi. **Quel âge a ton père? Et ta mère?** - Mon père a cinquante-deux ans et ma mère a trente-six ans.
4	**5**	**6**
Quel âge a ton père? - Mon père a soixante ans. **Quel âge a ta mère?** - Ma mère a cinquante-deux ans. **Tu t'entends bien avec ton père?** - Oui, je m'entends bien avec mon père, mais je ne m'entends pas bien avec ma mère.	**Quel âge a ton grand-père?** - Mon grand-père a soixante-dix ans. **Quel âge a ta grand-mère?** - Ma grand-mère a soixante-douze ans. **Tu t'entends bien avec ton grand-père?** - Non, je ne m'entends pas bien avec mon grand-père, mais je m'entends bien avec ma grand-mère.	**Quel âge a ton oncle Josh?** - Mon oncle Josh a soixante-trois ans. **Quel âge a ta tante Linda?** - Ma tante Linda a soixante-sept ans. **Tu t'entends bien avec ton oncle et ta tante?** - Je m'entends bien avec ma tante, mais je ne m'entends pas bien avec mon oncle.
7	**8**	**9**
Combien de personnes il y a dans ta famille? - Dans ma famille, il y a six personnes. Ma mère, mon père, mes deux sœurs, mon frère et moi. **Quel âge a ton père? Et ta mère?** - Mon père a quarante-huit ans et ma mère a trente-quatre ans.	**Quel âge a ton père?** - Mon père a soixante-quatre ans. **Quel âge a ta mère?** - Ma mère a cinquante-deux ans. **Tu t'entends bien avec tes parents?** - Oui et non. Je m'entends bien avec ma mère, mais je ne m'entends pas bien avec mon père.	**Comment tu t'appelles?** - Je m'appelle Charles. **D'où es-tu?** - Je suis de Londres, mais j'habite à Paris. **Combien de personnes il y a dans ta famille?** - Nous sommes quatre dans ma famille: mon père, ma mère, ma sœur et moi. **Tu t'entends bien avec tes parents?** - Je m'entends bien avec mon père, mais je ne m'entends pas bien avec ma mère.

UNIT 6 – SURVEY

	What is your name?	How old are you?	How many people are there in your family?	How old are your parents?	Do you get on with your father and mother?
	Comment tu t'appelles?	**Quel âge as-tu?**	**Combien de personnes il y a dans ta famille?**	**Quel âge ont tes parents?**	**Tu t'entends bien avec ton père et ta mère?**
e.g.	*Je m'appelle Marc.*	*J'ai onze ans.*	*Dans ma famille, il y a quatre personnes: ma mère, mon père, ma sœur et moi.*	*Ma mère a quarante ans et mon père a quarante-deux ans.*	*Je m'entends bien avec ma mère, mais je ne m'entends pas bien avec mon père.*
1.					
2.					
3.					
4.					
5.					
6.					
7.					

UNIT 6 – ANSWERS

FIND SOMEONE WHO

	Find someone whose father...	Name
1.	...is 43 years old.	Hugo
2.	...is 54 years old.	David
3.	...is 29 years old.	Alice
4.	...is 38 years old.	Antoinette
5.	...is 70 years old.	Nathan / Jeanne
6.	...is 34 years old.	Sonia
7.	...is 26 years old.	Daniel
8.	...is 42 years old.	Amélie
9.	...is 60 years old.	Mélanie
10.	...is 49 years old.	Claire
11.	...is 48 years old.	Fernand
12.	...is 58 years old.	Anna / Charles
13.	...is 37 years old.	Caroline
14.	...is 51 years old.	Béatrice

STAIRCASE TRANSLATION

Je m'appelle Suzanne. J'ai onze ans. Je suis de Paris. Dans ma famille, il y a quatre personnes: mon père, ma mère, mon frère et moi. Je m'entends bien avec mon père, mais je ne m'entends pas bien avec ma mère. Mon père a quarante ans et ma mère a trente-cinq ans. Ma sœur a quinze ans. Combien de personnes il y a dans ta famille? Quel âge a ton père? Quel âge a ta mère?

FASTER!

REFEREE SOLUTION:

1. Dans ma famille, il y a quatre personnes.
2. Mon père, ma mère, mon frère Julien et ma sœur Anna.
3. Mon père a trente-neuf ans.
4. Ma mère a quarante-trois ans.
5. Mon grand-père a soixante-et-onze ans.
6. Mon grand-père a soixante-quatre ans.
7. Je ne m'entends pas bien avec mon père.
8. Je m'entends bien avec ma mère.
9. Combien de personnes il y a dans ta famille?
10. Tu t'entends bien avec ta mère?

TRAPDOOR

1. Mon grand-père a quatre-vingts ans. Son anniversaire est le dix-huit août.
2. Ma cousine a quinze ans. Son anniversaire est le quinze janvier.
3. Mon frère a six ans. Son anniversaire est le vingt-deux juin.
4. Ma mère a trente-six ans. Son anniversaire est le neuf février.
5. Ma grand-mère a soixante-dix ans. Son anniversaire est le seize avril.
6. Mon père a cinquante ans. Son anniversaire est le trente septembre.
7. Ma sœur a vingt-six ans. Son anniversaire est le trente-et-un mars.

UNIT 7
Describing hair and eyes

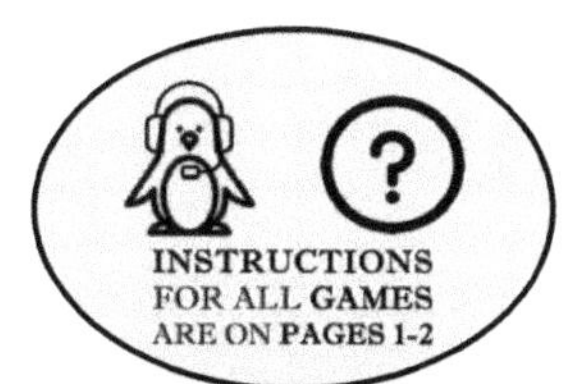

Comment tu t'appelles? *What is your name?*	**Comment sont tes cheveux?** *What is your hair like?*
Quel âge as-tu? *How old are you?*	**De quelle couleur sont tes yeux?** *What colour are your eyes?*

Comment il/elle s'appelle? *What is his/her name?*	**Comment sont ses cheveux?** *What is his/her hair like?*
Quel âge a-t-il/elle? *How old is he/she?*	**De quelle couleur sont ses yeux?** *What colour are his/her eyes?*

Je m'appelle... *I am called* **Il/Elle s'appelle** *He/She is called*	Anthony Charles Pierre Émilie Isabelle Marie Jules Julien Robert	**et** *and*	**j'ai** *I have* **il/elle a** *he/she has*	**six ans** *6 years* **sept ans** *7 years* **huit ans** *8 years* **neuf ans** *9 years* **dix ans** *10 years* **onze ans** *11 years* **douze ans** *12 years* **treize ans** *13 years* **quatorze ans** *14 years* **quinze ans** *15 years*	

J'ai les cheveux *I have...hair* **Il/Elle a les cheveux** *He/She has...hair*	**blonds** *blond* **bruns** *brown* **châtains** *light brown* **noirs** *black* **roux** *red*	**et**	**courts** *short* **en épis** *spiky* **frisés** *curly* **longs** *long* **mi-longs** *mid-length* **ondulés** *wavy* **raides** *straight* **rasés** *shaved*	

J'ai les yeux *I have... eyes* **Il/Elle a les yeux** *He/She has... eyes*	**bleu<u>s</u>** *blue* **marron** *brown* **noir<u>s</u>** *black* **vert<u>s</u>** *green*	**et**	**je porte** *I wear* **il/elle porte** *he/she wears*	**des lunettes** *glasses*
			j'ai *I have* **il a** *he has*	**une moustache** *a moustache* **une barbe** *a beard*

Author's note: in the negative form in French the "des" or "une" turns into "de"
Examples: -Je **ne** porte **pas de** lunettes. *I don't wear glasses.*
        -Je **n'**ai **pas de** moustache/barbe. *I don't have a moustache/beard.*
        -Elle **ne** porte **pas de** lunettes. *She doesn't wear glasses.*
        -Il **n'**a **pas de** moustache/barbe. *He doesn't have a moustache/beard.*

UNIT 7 – FIND SOMEONE WHO – Student Cards

J'ai les cheveux roux. J'ai les yeux marron. **SOPHIE**	J'ai les cheveux bruns. J'ai les yeux verts. **CAMILLE**	J'ai les cheveux châtains. J'ai les yeux bleus. **MATÉO**	J'ai les cheveux roux. J'ai les yeux bleus. **ALEXANDRE**
J'ai les cheveux bruns. J'ai les yeux verts. **VALENTINE**	J'ai les cheveux blonds. J'ai les yeux bleus. **ANNA**	J'ai les cheveux châtains. J'ai les yeux verts. **SYLVAIN**	J'ai les cheveux bruns. J'ai les yeux bleus. **ÉRIC**
J'ai les cheveux gris. J'ai les yeux bleus. **ISABELLE**	J'ai les cheveux blancs. J'ai les yeux bleus. **DANIEL**	J'ai les cheveux blonds. J'ai les yeux verts. **LÉONARD**	J'ai les cheveux blonds. J'ai les yeux marron. **PHILIPPE**
J'ai les cheveux bruns. J'ai les yeux bleus. **MARIE**	J'ai les cheveux châtains. J'ai les yeux gris. **LUCAS**	J'ai les cheveux châtains. J'ai les yeux verts. **SÉBASTIEN**	J'ai les cheveux bruns. J'ai les yeux gris. **PAUL**

UNIT 7 – FIND SOMEONE WHO – Student Grid

	Find someone who…	Name
1.	…has red hair and brown eyes.	
2.	…has light brown hair and grey eyes.	
3.	…has light brown hair and blue eyes.	
4.	…has red hair and blue eyes.	
5.	…has brown hair and green eyes.	
6.	…has blond hair and blue eyes.	
7.	…has light brown hair and green eyes.	
8.	…has brown hair and blue eyes.	
9.	…has grey hair and blue eyes.	
10.	…has white hair and blue eyes.	
11.	…has blond hair and green eyes.	
12.	…has blond hair and brown eyes.	
13.	…has brown hair and grey eyes.	

UNIT 7 – ORAL PING PONG – Person A

ENGLISH 1	FRENCH 1	ENGLISH 2	FRENCH 2
I have brown hair.	J'ai les cheveux bruns.	My grandfather has white hair and black eyes.	Mon grand-père a les cheveux blancs et les yeux noirs.
I have blue eyes.		My grandmother has white hair and blue eyes.	
I have blond hair.	J'ai les cheveux blonds.	I have red hair and blue eyes.	J'ai les cheveux roux et les yeux bleus.
I have medium-length hair.		I have brown hair and green eyes.	
I have straight dark brown hair.	J'ai les cheveux bruns et raides.	I have dark brown hair and brown eyes.	J'ai les cheveux bruns et les yeux marron.
I have curly red hair.		I have straight black hair and green eyes.	
I have blond hair and green eyes.	J'ai les cheveux blonds et les yeux verts.	I have curly blond hair and blue eyes.	J'ai les cheveux blonds et frisés et les yeux bleus.
My father has grey hair and green eyes.		I have wavy dark brown hair and black eyes.	
My mother has black hair and blue eyes.	Ma mère a les cheveux noirs et les yeux bleus.	I have straight blond hair and blue eyes.	J'ai les cheveux blonds et raides et les yeux bleus.
My sister has light brown hair and grey eyes.		I have short black hair and blue eyes.	

UNIT 7 – ORAL PING PONG – Person B

ENGLISH 1	FRENCH 1	ENGLISH 2	FRENCH 2
I have brown hair.		My grandfather has white hair and black eyes.	
I have blue eyes.	J'ai les yeux bleus.	My grandmother has white hair and blue eyes.	Ma grand-mère a les cheveux blancs et les yeux bleus.
I have blond hair.		I have red hair and blue eyes.	
I have medium-length hair.	J'ai les cheveux mi-longs.	I have brown hair and green yes.	J'ai les cheveux bruns et les yeux verts.
I have straight dark brown hair.		I have dark brown hair and brown eyes.	
I have curly red hair.	J'ai les cheveux roux et frisés.	I have straight black hair and green eyes.	J'ai les cheveux noirs et raides et les yeux verts.
I have blond hair and green eyes.		I have curly blond hair and blue eyes.	
My father has grey hair and green eyes.	Mon père a les cheveux gris et les yeux verts.	I have wavy dark brown hair and black eyes.	J'ai les cheveux bruns et ondulés et les yeux noirs.
My mother has black hair and blue eyes.		I have straight blond hair and blue eyes.	
My sister has light brown hair and grey eyes.	Ma sœur a les cheveux châtains et les yeux gris.	I have short black hair and blue eyes.	J'ai les cheveux noirs et courts et les yeux bleus.

No Snakes No Ladders

START	**1** What is your hair like?	**2** I wear glasses.	**3** I have short hair.	**4** What is your hair like?	**5** I have brown eyes.	**6** I have long hair.	**7** I have black eyes.
15 I have wavy hair.	**14** I have brown hair.	**13** I have short hair.	**12** What is your hair like?	**11** I have black eyes.	**10** I don't wear glasses.	**9** He has a beard.	**8** I have green eyes.
16 I have red and straight hair and I have green eyes.	**17** I have black and wavy hair and blue eyes.	**18** I have blond and curly hair and brown eyes.	**19** I have very long blond hair and green eyes.	**20** I have medium length hair and blue eyes.	**21** I have short blond hair.	**22** I have long black hair.	**23** I have very short hair.
FINISH	**30** My name is Pierre. I live in Nice. I have black and very short hair.	**29** My name is Anna. I live in Paris. I have red hair and brown eyes.	**28** I am twelve years old. I have green eyes and blond, straight hair.	**27** I am ten years old. I have blond and curly hair and blue eyes.	**26** I have curly light brown hair and green eyes. I wear glasses.	**25** I have long blond hair and grey eyes.	**24** I wear glasses and I have a moustache.

No Snakes No Ladders

DÉPART	1 Comment sont tes cheveux?	2 Je porte des lunettes.	3 J'ai les cheveux courts.	4 Comment sont tes cheveux?	5 J'ai les yeux marron.	6 J'ai les cheveux longs.	7 J'ai les yeux noirs.
15 J'ai les cheveux ondulés.	14 J'ai les cheveux bruns.	13 J'ai les cheveux courts.	12 Comment sont tes cheveux?	11 J'ai les yeux noirs.	10 Je ne porte pas de lunettes.	9 Il a une barbe.	8 J'ai les yeux verts.
16 J'ai les cheveux roux et raides et j'ai les yeux verts.	17 J'ai les cheveux noirs et ondulés et les yeux bleus.	18 J'ai les cheveux blonds et frisés et les yeux marron.	19 J'ai les cheveux blonds et très longs et les yeux verts.	20 J'ai les cheveux mi-longs et les yeux bleus.	21 J'ai les cheveux courts et blonds.	22 J'ai les cheveux longs et noirs.	23 J'ai les cheveux très courts.
ARRIVÉE	30 Je m'appelle Pierre. J'habite à Nice. J'ai les cheveux noirs et très courts.	29 Je m'appelle Anna. J'habite à Paris. J'ai les cheveux roux et les yeux marron.	28 J'ai douze ans. J'ai les yeux verts et les cheveux blonds et raides.	27 J'ai dix ans. J'ai les cheveux blonds et frisés et les yeux bleus.	26 J'ai les cheveux châtains et frisés et les yeux verts. Je porte des lunettes.	25 J'ai les cheveux longs et blonds et les yeux gris.	24 Je porte des lunettes et j'ai une moustache.

UNIT 7 – STAIRCASE TRANSLATION

My name is William. I am 12.

My name is William. I am 12. I am English but I live in France.

My name is William. I am 12. I am English but I live in France. I have long blond curly hair and blue eyes.

My name is William. I am 12. I am English but I live in France. I have long blond curly hair and blue eyes. My sister is called Susanne. She is 14.

My name is William. I am 12. I am English but I live in France. I have long blond curly hair and blue eyes. My sister is called Susanne. She is 14. She has short brown hair and green eyes. My girfriend is called Jade.

* My name is William. I am 12. I am English but I live in France. I have long blond curly hair and blue eyes. My sister is called Susanne. She is 14. She has short brown hair and green eyes. My girfriend is called Jade. She is 13. She has red medium length curly hair and she has green eyes.

* Translate the
last step here:

# ⏱ UNIT 7 – FASTER! 🚀

Say:

1. I have blond hair and blue eyes.
2. I have black hair and green eyes.
3. I have brown hair and grey eyes.
4. I have red hair and I have brown eyes.
5. My brother has red and straight hair.
6. My sister has blond and curly hair.
7. My girlfriend has black and curly hair and blue eyes.
8. My father has long red straight hair and brown eyes.
9. I am twelve years old. I have green eyes and blond, straight hair.
10. He is fifteen years old. He has black, curly long hair and green eyes.

	Time	Mistakes	Referee's name
1			
2			
3			
4			

 # UNIT 7 – DETECTIVES & INFORMANTS 

DETECTIVES	Français		English	
	Cheveux	Yeux	Hair	Eyes
Comment est l'oncle de Marie?				
Comment est le frère aîné de Marie?				
Comment est la tante de Marie?				
La mère de Marie est brune ou blonde? Et ses yeux?				
Le père de Marie est roux ou brun? Et ses yeux?				
Comment est le frère cadet de Marie?				
Comment est le grand-père de Marie?				
Comment est la grand-mère de Marie?				

INFORMANTS

L'oncle de Marie a les cheveux blonds et les yeux bleus.	Le père de Marie a les cheveux bruns et courts et il a les yeux marron.
Le frère aîné de Marie a les cheveux noirs et les yeux marron.	Le frère cadet de Marie a les cheveux châtains et mi-longs et il a les yeux verts.
La tante de Marie a les cheveux roux et les yeux verts.	Le grand-père de Marie a les cheveux blancs et courts et les yeux bleus.
La mère de Marie a les cheveux longs et blonds et les yeux bleus.	La grand-mère de Marie a les cheveux gris et frisés. Elle a les yeux marron.

UNIT 7 – COMMUNICATIVE DRILLS

1	2	3
What is your hair like? - I have blond, long and curly hair. **What colour are your eyes?** - I have blue eyes.	**What is your hair like?** - I have black, long and curly hair. **What colour are your eyes?** - I have green eyes.	**What is your hair like?** - I have red, short and curly hair. **What colour are your eyes?** - I have brown eyes.
4	**5**	**6**
What is your hair like? - I have light brown, long and straight hair. **What colour are your eyes?** - I have black eyes.	**What is your hair like?** - I have black, long, wavy hair. **What colour are your eyes?** - I have brown eyes.	**What is your hair like?** - I have white and shaved hair. **What colour are your eyes?** - I have green eyes.
7	**8**	**9**
What is his hair like? - He has blond, medium length and curly hair. **What colour are his eyes?** - He has blue eyes.	**What is her hair like?** - She has red, medium length and straight hair. **What colour are her eyes?** - She has green eyes.	**What is her hair like?** - She has brown, long and straight hair. **What colour are her eyes?** - She has green eyes.

UNIT 7 – COMMUNICATIVE DRILLS
REFEREE CARD

1	2	3
Comment sont tes cheveux? - J'ai les cheveux blonds, longs et frisés. **De quelle couleur sont tes yeux?** - J'ai les yeux bleus.	**Comment sont tes cheveux?** - J'ai les cheveux bruns, longs et frisés. **De quelle couleur sont tes yeux?** - J'ai les yeux verts.	**Comment sont tes cheveux?** - J'ai les cheveux roux, courts et frisés. **De quelle couleur sont tes yeux?** - J'ai les yeux marron.
4	**5**	**6**
Comment sont tes cheveux? - J'ai les cheveux châtains, longs et raides. **De quelle couleur sont tes yeux?** - J'ai les yeux noirs.	**Comment sont tes cheveux?** - J'ai les cheveux noirs, longs et ondulés. **De quelle couleur sont tes yeux?** - J'ai les yeux marron.	**Comment sont tes cheveux?** - J'ai les cheveux blancs et rasés. **De quelle couleur sont tes yeux?** - J'ai les yeux verts.
7	**8**	**9**
Comment sont ses cheveux? - Il a les cheveux blonds, mi-longs et frisés. **De quelle couleur sont ses yeux?** - Il a les yeux bleus.	**Comment sont ses cheveux?** - Elle a les cheveux roux, mi-longs et raides. **De quelle couleur sont ses yeux?** - Elle a les yeux verts.	**Comment sont ses cheveux?** - Elle a les cheveux bruns, longs et raides. **De quelle couleur sont ses yeux?** - Elle a les yeux verts.

UNIT 7 – SURVEY

	What is your name?	How old are you?	How many people are there in your family?	What is your hair like?	What colour are your eyes?	And your mother? What is her hair like? What colour are her eyes?
	Comment tu t'appelles?	Quel âge as-tu?	Combien de personnes il y a dans ta famille?	Comment sont tes cheveux?	De quelle couleur sont tes yeux?	Et ta mère? Comment sont ses cheveux? De quelle couleur sont ses yeux?
e.g.	*Je m'appelle Marc.*	*J'ai onze ans.*	*Dans ma famille, il y a quatre personnes: ma mère, mon père, ma sœur et moi.*	*J'ai les cheveux châtains, courts et frisés.*	*J'ai les yeux marron.*	*Ma mère a les cheveux blonds et longs et elle a les yeux bleus.*
1.						
2.						
3.						
4.						
5.						
6.						
7.						

UNIT 7 – ANSWERS

FIND SOMEONE WHO

	Find someone who...	Name
1.	...has red hair and brown eyes.	Sophie
2.	...has light brown hair and grey eyes.	Lucas
3.	...has light brown hair and blue eyes.	Matéo
4.	...has red hair and blue eyes.	Alexandre
5.	...has brown hair and green eyes.	Valentine / Camille
6.	...has blond hair and blue eyes.	Anna
7.	...has light brown hair and green eyes.	Sylvain / Sébastien
8.	...has brown hair and blue eyes.	Éric / Marie
9.	...has grey hair and blue eyes.	Isabelle
10.	...has white hair and blue eyes.	Daniel
11.	...has blond hair and green eyes.	Léonard
12.	...has blond hair and brown eyes.	Philippe
13.	...has brown hair and grey eyes.	Paul

STAIRCASE TRANSLATION

Je m'appelle William. J'ai douze ans. Je suis anglais, mais j'habite en France. J'ai les cheveux longs, blonds et frisés et les yeux bleus. Ma sœur s'appelle Susanne. Elle a quatorze ans. Elle a les cheveux courts et bruns et les yeux verts. Ma petite amie s'appelle Jade. Elle a treize ans. Elle a les cheveux roux, mi-longs et frisés et elle a les yeux verts.

FASTER!

REFEREE SOLUTION:

1. J'ai les cheveux blonds et les yeux bleus.
2. J'ai les cheveux noirs et les yeux verts.
3. J'ai les cheveux bruns et les yeux gris.
4. J'ai les cheveux roux et j'ai les yeux marron.
5. Mon frère a les cheveux roux et raides.
6. Ma sœur a les cheveux blonds et frisés.
7. Ma petite amie a les cheveux noirs et frisés et les yeux bleus.
8. Mon père a les cheveux longs, roux et raides et les yeux marron.
9. J'ai douze ans. J'ai les yeux verts et les cheveux blonds et raides.
10. Il a quinze ans. Il a les cheveux longs, noirs et frisés et les yeux verts.

DETECTIVES & INFORMANTS

DETECTIVES	Français		English	
	Cheveux	**Yeux**	**Hair**	**Eyes**
Comment est l'oncle de Marie?	Blonds	Bleus	Blond	Blue
Comment est le frère aîné de Marie?	Noirs	Marron	Black	Brown
Comment est la tante de Marie?	Roux	Verts	Red	Green
La mère de Marie est brune ou blonde? Et ses yeux?	(Elle est) blonde	Bleus	(The mother is) blonde	Blue
Le père de Marie est roux ou brun? Et ses yeux?	(Il est) brun	Marron	Brown	Brown
Comment est le frère cadet de Marie?	Châtains, mi-longs	Verts	Light brown, mid length	Green
Comment est le grand-père de Marie?	Blancs, courts	Bleus	White, short	Blue
Comment est la grand-mère de Marie?	Gris, frisés	Marron	Grey, curly	Brown

UNIT 8
Describing myself and another family member

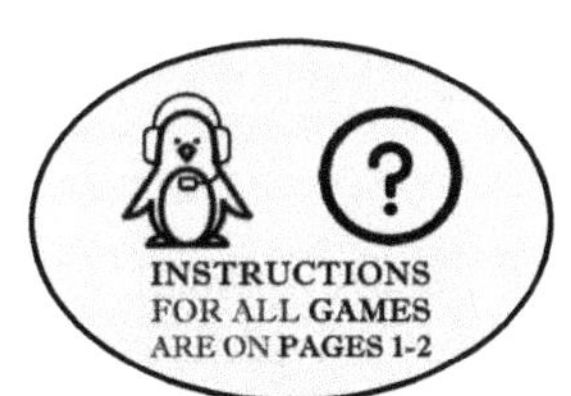

Combien de personnes il y a dans ta famille?	*How many people are there in your family?*
Comment est ton père/ta mère?	*What is your father/mother like?*
Tu t'entends bien avec ton frère/ta sœur?	*Do you get on well with your brother/sister?*

Dans ma famille, il y a quatre personnes	*In my family, there are four people*
Il y a cinq personnes dans ma famille	*There are five people in my family*

Dans ma famille j'ai *In my family I have…*	**mon grand-père, Claude** *my grandfather Claude* **mon père, Georges** *my father Georges* **mon oncle, Paul** *my uncle Paul* **mon petit/grand frère, Olivier** *my little/big brother Olivier* **mon cousin, Tristan** *my -boy- cousin Tristan*	**car/ parce qu'** *because*	**il est** *he is*	**assez** *quite* **très** *very* **un peu** *a bit*	**amusant** *fun* **beau** *handsome* **fort** *strong* **généreux** *generous* **grand** *tall* **gros** *fat* **honnête** *honest* **intelligent** *clever* **méchant** *mean* **mince** *slim* **petit** *short* **sympa** *nice* **timide** *shy* **têtu** *stubborn*
Dans ma famille il y a <u>quatre</u> personnes *There are <u>four</u> people in my family…*					
Je m'entends bien avec… *I get along well with…*	**ma grand-mère, Thérèse** *my grandmother Thérèse* **ma mère, Éliane** *my mother Éliane* **ma tante, Françoise** *my aunt Françoise* **ma petite/grande sœur, Léa** *my little/big sister Léa* **ma cousine, Claire** *my -girl- cousin Claire*		**elle est** *she is*		**amusante** **belle** **forte** **généreuse** **grande** **grosse** **honnête** **intelligente** **méchante** **mince** **petite** **sympa** **timide** **têtue**
Je m'entends mal avec… *I get along badly with…*					

UNIT 8 – FIND SOMEONE WHO – Student Cards

Mon père est grand. Ma mère est amusante. **ÉDOUARD**	Mon père est têtu. Ma mère est intelligente. **ALAIN**	Mon père est beau. Ma mère est honnête. **RÉGINE**	Mon père est sympa Ma mère est généreuse. **CAROLINE**
Mon père est très fort. Ma mère est timide. **XAVIER**	Mon père est amusant. Ma mère est patiente. **ROBERT**	Mon père est têtu. Ma mère est mince. **THÉRÈSE**	Mon père est assez fort. Ma mère est assez petite. **YVAN**
Mon père est un peu gros. Ma mère est grande. **JULIEN**	Mon père est intelligent. Ma mère n'est pas patiente. **ESTELLE**	Mon père est gros. Ma mère est mince. **JADE**	Mon père est méchant. Ma mère est sympa. **CARMEN**
Mon père est très fort. Ma mère est belle. **ADRIEN**	Mon père est mince. Ma mère est sympa. **MARINE**	Mon père est petit. Ma mère est grande. **ANTHONY**	Mon père est généreux. Ma mère est grande. **ALEXANDRA**

UNIT 8 – FIND SOMEONE WHO – Student Grid

	Find someone who...	**Name**
1.	...has a tall father.	
2.	...has an intelligent mother.	
3.	...has a good-looking father.	
4.	...has a fun mother.	
5.	...has a very strong father.	
6.	...has a fun father.	
7.	...has a stubborn father.	
8.	...has a mother who is quite short.	
9.	...has a generous mother.	
10.	...has an intelligent father.	
11.	...has a slim mother.	
12.	...has a nice mother.	
13.	...has a tall mother.	

UNIT 8 – ORAL PING PONG – Person A

ENGLISH 1	FRENCH 1	ENGLISH 2	FRENCH 2
I like my father because he is nice.	J'aime mon père car il est sympa.	I don't like my younger brother because he is mean.	Je n'aime pas mon frère cadet car il est méchant.
I don't like my mother because she is stubborn.		My aunt Léa is short, slim and beautiful.	
I like my dog because he is fun.	J'aime mon chien parce qu'il est amusant.	My uncle Pierre is tall and fat.	Mon oncle Pierre est grand et gros.
I like my cat because he is fat.		My younger sister is short, but strong.	
I like my younger brother because he is fun.	J'aime mon frère cadet car il est amusant.	My older brother is very handsome and strong.	Mon frère aîné est très beau et fort.
I like my older sister because she is intelligent.		My younger sister is short and slim.	
I get on well with my father because he is nice.	Je m'entends bien avec mon père car il est sympa.	My father is tall and a bit fat.	Mon père est grand et un peu gros.
I get on badly with my mother because she is mean.		My mother is intelligent and nice, but a bit stubborn.	
I don't get on well with my brother because he is stubborn.	Je ne m'entends pas bien avec mon frère car il est têtu.	My grandfather is tall, slim and handsome.	Mon grand-père est grand, mince et beau.
I like my mother because she is nice.		My grandmother is very nice and intelligent.	

UNIT 8 – ORAL PING PONG – Person B

ENGLISH 1	FRENCH 1	ENGLISH 2	FRENCH 2
I like my father because he is nice.		I don't like my younger brother because he is mean.	
I don't like my mother because she is stubborn.	Je n'aime pas ma mère car elle est têtue.	My aunt Léa is short, slim and beautiful.	Ma tante Léa est petite, mince et belle.
I like my dog because he is fun.		My uncle Pierre is tall and fat.	
I like my cat because he is fat.	J'aime mon chat parce qu'il est gros.	My younger sister is short, but strong.	Ma sœur cadette est petite, mais forte.
I like my younger brother because he is fun.		My older brother is very handsome and strong.	
I like my older sister because she is intelligent.	J'aime ma sœur aînée car elle est intelligente.	My younger sister is short and slim.	Ma sœur cadette est petite et mince.
I get on well with my father because he is nice.		My father is tall and a bit fat.	
I get on badly with my mother because she is mean.	Je m'entends mal avec ma mère car elle est méchante.	My mother is intelligent and nice, but a bit stubborn.	Ma mère est intelligente et sympa, mais un peu têtue.
I don't get on well with my brother because he is stubborn.		My grandfather is tall, slim and handsome.	
I like my mother because she is nice.	J'aime ma mère parce qu'elle est sympa.	My grandmother is very nice and intelligent.	Ma grand-mère est très sympa et intelligente.

No Snakes No Ladders

START

1. Do you like your cousin Pierre?
2. Do you like your cousin Suzanne?
3. Why do you like your aunt Anna?
4. Why don't you get on well with your father?
5. I get on well with my mother because she is very nice.
6. I like my brother because he is fun.
7. I don't like my uncle Marc because he is mean.
8. I like my uncle because is tall and strong.
9. I like my mother because she is intelligent and nice.
10. I like my father a lot because he is fun, intelligent and nice.
11. Why don't you get on well with your mother?
12. Why don't you like your aunt Anna?
13. Do you like your cousin Paul?
14. My brother is tall. My sister is short.
15. My mother is very slim. My father is a bit fat.
16. My aunt is very nice. My uncle is mean.
17. My father is 47. He is tall and strong. He is very nice.
18. Do you get on well with your grandfather?
19. Do you like your uncle Charles?
20. I get on badly with my cousin because he is mean and stubborn.
21. My cousin Marianne is tall and strong. She is also very nice.
22. My mother is short, slim and strong. She is also very fun.
23. My grandfather is 70. He is very tall.
24. My father is 38. He is short and a bit fat but handsome.
25. My older brother is called Philippe. He is 16. He is tall and slim.
26. My uncle Michel is very handsome, but he is very mean and stubborn.
27. Why don't you get on well with your father?
28. Do you get on well with your parents?
29. I get on well with my mother because she is very nice.
30. I love my father because he is fun, intelligent and nice.

FINISH

No Snakes No Ladders

DÉPART	1 Tu aimes ton cousin Pierre?	2 Tu aimes ta cousine Suzanne?	3 Pourquoi tu aimes ta tante Anna?	4 Pourquoi tu ne t'entends pas bien avec ton père?	5 Je m'entends bien avec ma mère car elle est très sympa.	6 J'aime mon frère car il est amusant.	7 Je n'aime pas mon oncle Marc car il est méchant.
15 Ma mère est très mince. Mon père est un peu gros.	14 Mon frère est grand. Ma sœur est petite.	13 Tu aimes ton cousin Paul?	12 Pourquoi tu n'aimes pas ta tante Anna?	11 Pourquoi tu ne t'entends pas bien avec ta mère?	10 J'aime beaucoup mon père car il est amusant, intelligent et sympa.	9 J'aime ma mère car elle est intelligente et sympa.	8 J'aime mon oncle car il est grand et fort.
16 Ma tante est très sympa. Mon oncle est méchant.	17 Mon père a quarante-sept ans. Il est grand et fort. Il est très sympa.	18 Tu t'entends bien avec ton grand-père?	19 Tu t'entends avec ton oncle Charles?	20 Je m'entends mal avec mon cousin car il est méchant et têtu.	21 Ma cousine Marianne est grande et forte. Elle est aussi très sympa	22 Ma mère est petite, mince et forte. Elle est aussi très amusante.	23 Mon grand-père a soixante-dix ans. Il est très grand.
ARRIVÉE	30 J'adore mon père car il est amusant, intelligent et sympa.	29 Je m'entends bien avec ma mère car elle est très sympa.	28 Tu t'entends bien avec tes parents?	27 Pourquoi tu ne t'entends pas bien avec ton père?	26 Mon oncle Michel est très beau, mais il est très méchant et têtu.	25 Mon frère aîné s'appelle Philippe. Il a seize ans. Il est grand et mince.	24 Mon père a trente-huit ans. Il est petit et un peu gros, mais beau.

UNIT 8 – STAIRCASE TRANSLATION

I don't like my uncle Joël because he is mean...

I don't like my uncle Joël because he is mean and stubborn...

I don't like my uncle Joël because he is mean and stubborn but I love my aunt Miriam because she is honest and generous.

I don't like my uncle Joël because he is mean and stubborn but I love my aunt Myriam because she is honest and generous. I like my cousin Pierre because he is very nice and fun.

I don't like my uncle Joël because he is mean and stubborn but I love my aunt Myriam because she is honest and generous. I like my cousin Pierre because he is very nice and fun, but I get on badly with my cousin Alexandra because she is very mean and arrogant.

* I don't like my uncle Joël because he is mean and stubborn but I love my aunt Myriam because she is honest and generous. I like my cousin Pierre because he is very nice and fun, but I get on badly with my cousin Alexandra because she is very mean and arrogant. And you, do you get on well with your uncles, your aunts and your cousins?

* Translate the last step here:

⏱ UNIT 8 – FASTER! 🪐

Say:

1. I like my father a lot.
2. I love my mother.
3. My mother is tall and slim.
4. My dog is fat and fun.
5. My brother is nice and fun.
6. My sister is strong and mean.
7. My uncle is very nice.
8. My aunt is very stubborn.
9. My grandmother is generous.
10. Do you get on with your cousin Angela?

	Time	Mistakes	Referee's name
1			
2			
3			
4			

 # UNIT 8 – FAST & FURIOUS 

1. Mon frère est _______________ .   *tall*

2. Ma meilleure amie est _______________ .   *nice*

3. Ma tortue est _______________ .   *fun*

4. Mon cousin est _______________ .   *shy*

5. Mon grand-père est _______________ .   *generous*

6. Mon chat est _______________ .   *intelligent*

7. Mon oncle est _______________ .   *stubborn*

8. Mon frère aîné est _______________ .   *good looking*

9. Ma sœur est _______________ .   *mean*

10. Mon chien est _______________ .   *fat*

	Time 1	Time 2	Time 3	Time 4
Time				
Mistakes				

UNIT 8 – COMMUNICATIVE DRILLS

1	2	3
Do you get on well with your father? - Yes, I get on well with my father because he is nice and patient. **Do you get on well with your mother?** - No, I don't get on well with my mother because she is very strict *(stricte)*.	**Do you get on well with your mother?** - Yes, I get on well with my mother because she is quite nice and generous. **Do you get on well with your father?** - No, I don't get on well with my father because he is very mean.	**Do you get on well with your older brother?** - Yes, I get on well with my older brother because he is nice, patient and generous. **Do you get on well with your younger brother?** - No, I don't get on well with my younger brother because he is very arrogant, mean and stubborn.

4	5	6
What is your mother like? - Physically, *(Physiquement)* she is very tall, a bit fat, but good-looking. In terms of personality, *(En termes de personnalité)* she is nice, very generous and patient.	**What is your father like?** - Physically, he is not very tall. He is slim and quite strong. In terms of personality, he is nice, patient and honest.	**What is your grandmother like?** - Physically, she is very short and a quite slim. In terms of personality, she is very nice, generous and a bit shy.

7	8	9
Why don't you like your cousin Fernand? - I don't like my cousin Fernand because he is very mean and stubborn. **Do you like your cousin Marie-Hélène?** - Yes, because she is clever and fun.	**Why don't you like your uncle Serge?** - I don't like my uncle Serge because he is very arrogant and not very clever. **Do you like your aunt Suzanne?** - Yes, because she is very nice and generous.	**Why don't you like your maths teacher?** - I don't like my maths teacher because he is mean. **Do you like your science teacher?** - Yes, because she is very nice and patient.

UNIT 8 – COMMUNICATIVE DRILLS
REFEREE CARD

1	2	3
Tu t'entends bien avec ton père? - Oui, je m'entends bien avec mon père car il est sympa et patient. **Tu t'entends bien avec ta mère?** - Non, je ne m'entends pas bien avec ma mère car elle est très stricte.	**Tu t'entends bien avec ta mère?** - Oui, je m'entends bien avec ma mère car elle est assez sympa et généreuse. **Tu t'entends bien avec ton père?** - Non, je ne m'entends pas bien avec mon père car il est très méchant.	**Tu t'entends bien avec ton frère aîné?** - Oui je m'entends bien avec mon frère aîné parce qu'il est sympa, patient et généreux. **Tu t'entends bien avec ton frère cadet?** - Non, je ne m'entends pas bien avec mon frère cadet car il est très arrogant, méchant et têtu.
4	**5**	**6**
Comment est ta mère? - Physiquement, elle est très grande, un peu grosse, mais belle. En termes de personnalité, elle est sympa, très généreuse et patiente.	**Comment est ton père?** - Physiquement, il n'est pas très grand. Il est mince et assez fort. En termes de personnalité, il est sympa, patient et honnête.	**Comment est ta grand-mère?** - Physiquement, elle est très petite et assez mince. En termes de personnalité, elle est très sympa, généreuse et un peu timide.
7	**8**	**9**
Pourquoi tu n'aimes pas ton cousin Fernand? - Je n'aime pas mon cousin Fernand car il est très méchant et têtu. **Tu aimes ta cousine Marie-Hélène?** - Oui, parce qu'elle est intelligente et amusante.	**Pourquoi tu n'aimes pas ton oncle Serge?** - Je n'aime pas mon oncle Serge car il est très arrogant et il n'est pas très intelligent. **Tu aimes ta tante Suzanne?** - Oui, parce qu'elle est très sympa et généreuse.	**Pourquoi tu n'aimes pas ton prof de maths?** - Je n'aime pas mon professeur de mathématiques car il est méchant. **Tu aimes ta professeure de sciences?** - Oui parce qu'elle est très sympa et patiente.

UNIT 8 – SURVEY

	What is your name?	How many people are there in your family?	What is your father like?	Do you get on well with your mother?	Do you get on well with your brother/sister?
	Comment tu t'appelles?	Combien de personnes il y a dans ta famille?	Comment est ton père?	Tu t'entends bien avec ta mère?	Tu t'entends bien avec ta sœur?
e.g.	*Je m'appelle Anna.*	*Dans ma famille, il y a quatre personnes: mon père, ma mère, mon frère et moi.*	*Il est très sympa et généreux.*	*Oui, je m'entends bien avec ma mère car elle est très patiente.*	*Oui, je m'entends bien avec ma sœur car elle est très amusante et sympa.*
1.					
2.					
3.					
4.					
5.					
6.					
7.					

UNIT 8 – ANSWERS

FIND SOMEONE WHO

	Find someone who...	Name
1.	...has a tall father.	Édouard
2.	...has an intelligent mother.	Alain
3.	...has a good-looking father.	Régine
4.	...has a fun mother.	Édouard
5.	...has a very strong father.	Xavier / Adrien
6.	...has a fun father.	Robert
7.	...has a stubborn father.	Thérèse
8.	...has a mother who is quite short.	Yvan
9.	...has a generous mother.	Caroline
10.	...has an intelligent father.	Estelle
11.	...has a slim mother.	Thérèse / Jade
12.	...has a nice mother.	Marine / Carmen
13.	...has a tall mother.	Anthony / Julien / Alexandra

STAIRCASE TRANSLATION

Je n'aime pas mon oncle Joël car il est méchant et têtu, mais j'adore ma tante Myriam car elle est honnête et généreuse. J'aime mon cousin Pierre car il est très sympa et amusant, mais je m'entends mal avec ma cousine Alexandra car elle est très méchante et arrogante. Et toi? Tu t'entends bien avec tes oncles, tes tantes et tes cousins?

FASTER!

REFEREE SOLUTION:

1. J'aime beaucoup mon père.
2. J'adore ma mère.
3. Ma mère est grande et mince.
4. Mon chien est gros et amusant.
5. Mon frère est sympa et amusant.
6. Ma sœur est forte et méchante.
7. Mon oncle est très sympa.
8. Ma tante est très têtue.
9. Ma grand-mère est généreuse.
10. Tu t'entends bien avec ta cousine Angela?

FAST & FURIOUS

1. Mon frère est **grand**.
2. Ma meilleure amie est **sympa**.
3. Ma tortue est **amusante**.
4. Mon cousin est **timide**.
5. Mon grand-père est **généreux**.
6. Mon chat est **intelligent**.
7. Mon oncle est **têtu**.
8. Mon frère aîné est **beau**.
9. Ma sœur est **méchante**.
10. Mon chien est **gros**.

UNIT 9
Comparing people

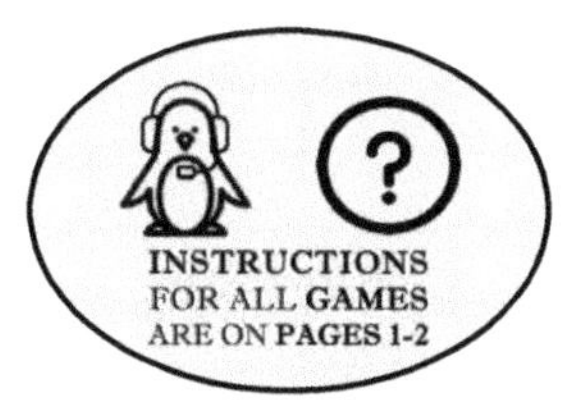

INSTRUCTIONS FOR ALL GAMES ARE ON PAGES 1-2

Elle					
Il			affectueux/euse(s) *affectionate*		ma grand-mère
Ma grand-mère			aimable(s) *likeable*		mon grand-père
Mon grand-père			amusant(e)(s) *funny*		mon amie Anne
Mon amie Anne			antipathique(s) *unfriendly*		mon ami Paul
Mon ami Paul			barbant(e)(s) *boring*		mon chat
Mon chat			bavard(e)(s) *talkative*		ma sœur
Ma sœur			beau(x)/belle(s)		mon frère
Mon frère			*good-looking*		mon fils
Mon fils			bruyant(e)(s) *noisy*		ma fille
Ma fille		**plus**	faible(s) *weak*		ma mère
Ma mère		*more*	fort(e)(s) *strong*		ma meilleure amie
Ma meilleure amie	**est**		grand(e)(s) *tall*		mon meilleur ami
Mon meilleur ami	*is*		gros/se(s) *fat*	**que**	mon père
Mon père		**moins**	intelligent(e)(s) *intelligent*	*than /*	mon canard
Mon canard	**sont**	*less*	jeune(s) *young*	*as*	mon chien
Mon chien	*are*		mince(s) *slim*		ma cousine
Ma cousine			moche(s) *ugly*		mon cousin
Mon cousin		**aussi**	paresseux/euse(s) *lazy*		ma tortue
Ma tortue		*as*	petit(e)(s) *short*		ma tante
Ma tante			sérieux/euse(s) *serious*		mon oncle
Mon oncle			sportif/ive(s) *sporty*		mes grands-parents
Mes grands-parents			stupide(s) *stupid*		mes sœurs
Mes sœurs			sympa *nice*		mes frères
Mes frères			tranquille(s) *relaxed*		ma petite amie
Ma petite amie *(gf)*			travailleur/euse(s) *hard-working*		mon petit ami
Mon petit ami *(bf)*			vieux/vieille(s) *old*		mes parents
Mes parents					mes oncles
Mes oncles					moi

UNIT 9 – FIND SOMEONE WHO – Student Cards

Ma sœur est plus petite que mon frère. **OSCAR**	Ma sœur est plus bavarde que mon frère. **ROMAIN**	Mon frère est plus sympa que ma sœur. **ISABELLE**	Mon chien est plus barbant que mon chat. **FERNAND**
Ma sœur est aussi forte que mon frère. **VICTOR**	Ma sœur est plus tranquille que mon frère. **MARTIN**	Mon chat est plus gros que mon chien. **HÉLÈNE**	Ma sœur est moins bruyante que mon frère. **SONIA**
Mon chat est plus moche que mon chien. **SERGE**	Mon frère cadet est plus petit que mon frère aîné. **PAUL**	Ma sœur est aussi travailleuse que mon frère. **LÉA**	Ma sœur est plus sympa que mon frère. **RAPHAËL**
Mon frère est plus paresseux qu'un paresseux. **JULIEN**	Mon chien est plus bruyant que mon chat. **PATRICIA**	Ma sœur est plus sportive que mon frère. **ROSANNE**	Mon chien est aussi stupide que mon chat. **MARIE**

UNIT 9 – FIND SOMEONE WHO – Student Grid

	Find someone whose...	Name
1.	...sister is sportier than their brother.	
2.	...sister is more talkative than their brother.	
3.	...brother is nicer than their sister.	
4.	...dog is more boring than their cat.	
5.	...sister is as strong as their brother.	
6.	...sister is more relaxed than their brother.	
7.	...cat is fatter than their dog.	
8.	...sister is less noisy than their brother.	
9.	...cat is uglier than their dog.	
10.	...younger brother is shorter than their older brother.	
11.	...sister is as hard-working as their brother.	
12.	...sister is nicer than their brother.	
13.	...brother is lazier than a sloth.	
14.	...dog is noisier than their cat.	
15.	...dog is as stupid as their cat.	
16	...sister is shorter than their brother.	

UNIT 9 – ORAL PING PONG – Person A

ENGLISH 1	FRENCH 1	ENGLISH 2	FRENCH 2
My grandfather is taller than my father.	Mon grand-père est plus grand que mon père.	She is more boring than him.	Elle est plus barbante que lui.
My sister is shorter than me.		My friend Anna is weaker than me.	
My best friend (f) is less hard-working than me.	Ma meilleure amie est moins travailleuse que moi.	My friend Paul is less tall than me.	Mon ami Paul est moins grand que moi.
My son is more handsome than me.		My turtle is more intelligent than my dog.	
My mother is as talkative as my sister.	Ma mère est aussi bavarde que ma sœur.	My grandmother is younger than my grandfather.	Ma grand-mère est plus jeune que mon grand-père.
My dog is noisier than my cat.		My uncle is older than my father.	
My older brother is less affectionate than my younger brother.	Mon frère aîné est moins affectueux que mon frère cadet.	My brother is less nice than my sister.	Mon frère est moins sympa que ma sœur.
My mother is prettier than my aunt.		My mother is more serious than my father.	
My father is sportier than me.	Mon père est plus sportif que moi.	My aunt is older than my uncle.	Ma tante est plus vieille que mon oncle.
My best friend (m) is as strong as me.		My cousin (f) is more stupid than my sister.	

UNIT 9 – ORAL PING PONG – Person B

ENGLISH 1	FRENCH 1	ENGLISH 2	FRENCH 2
My grandfather is taller than my father.		**She is more boring than him.**	
My sister is shorter than me.	Ma sœur est plus petite que moi.	**My friend Anna is weaker than me.**	Mon amie Anna est plus faible que moi.
My best friend (f) is less hard-working than me.		**My friend Paul is less tall than me.**	
My son is more handsome than me.	Mon fils est plus beau que moi.	**My turtle is more intelligent than my dog.**	Ma tortue est plus intelligente que mon chien.
My mother is as talkative as my sister.		**My grandmother is younger than my grandfather.**	
My dog is noisier than my cat.	Mon chien est plus bruyant que mon chat.	**My uncle is older than my father.**	Mon oncle est plus vieux que mon père.
My older brother is less affectionate than my younger brother.		**My brother is less nice than my sister.**	
My mother is prettier than my aunt.	Ma mère est plus belle que ma tante	**My mother is more serious than my father.**	Ma mère est plus sérieuse que mon père.
My father is sportier than me.		**My aunt is older than my uncle.**	
My best friend (m) is as strong as me.	Mon meilleur ami est aussi fort que moi.	**My cousin (f) is more stupid than my sister.**	Ma cousine est plus stupide que ma sœur.

No Snakes No Ladders

7 — My grandfather is younger than my grandmother.	6 — I am slimmer (f) than my sister.	5 — My older brother is stronger than my father.	4 — My best friend (f) is stronger than my best friend Jean.	3 — Who is younger, your father or your uncle?	2 — Who is taller, your brother or your sister?	1 — My sister is taller than me.
8 — My brother is lazier than me.	9 — My aunt is nicer than my uncle.	10 — My father is as talkative as me.	11 — He is less sporty than her.	12 — My dog is less intelligent than my cat.	13 — My father is more serious than my mother.	14 — My cat is less noisy than my dog.
23 — My girlfriend is as beautiful as her.	22 — My parents are as good-looking as me.	21 — I am less boring (m) than her.	20 — I am as lazy (m) as him.	19 — I am less ugly (m) than my brother.	18 — I am as hard-working (m) as my father.	17 — My mother is more relaxed than my father.
24 — He is less affectionate than her.	25 — My uncle is less nice than my aunt.	26 — My parents are more hard-working than my grandparents.	27 — My parents are less nice than my grandparents.	28 — My brother is shorter than me but he is stronger.	29 — I am not as strong as my brother, but I am more handsome than him.	30 — I am not as intelligent as my father, but I am stronger than him.

START

15 — My best friend (M) is taller than me.

16 — My turtle is less stupid than my brother.

FINISH

No Snakes No Ladders

DÉPART	1 Ma sœur est plus grande que moi.	2 Qui est plus grand, ton frère ou ta sœur?	3 Qui est plus jeune, ton père ou ton oncle?	4 Ma meilleure amie est plus forte que mon meilleur ami Jean.	5 Mon frère aîné est plus fort que mon père.	6 Je suis plus mince que ma sœur.	7 Mon grand-père est plus jeune que ma grand-mère.
15 Mon meilleur ami est plus grand que moi.	14 Mon chat est moins bruyant que mon chien.	13 Mon père est moins sérieux que ma mère.	12 Mon chien est moins intelligent que mon chat.	11 Il est moins sportif qu'elle.	10 Mon père est aussi bavard que moi.	9 Ma tante est plus sympa que mon oncle.	8 Mon frère est plus paresseux que moi.
16 Ma tortue est moins stupide que mon frère.	17 Ma mère est plus tranquille que mon père.	18 Je suis aussi travailleur que mon père.	19 Je suis moins moche que mon frère.	20 Je suis aussi paresseux que lui.	21 Je suis moins barbant qu'elle.	22 Mes parents sont aussi beaux que moi.	23 Ma petite amie est aussi belle qu'elle.
ARRIVÉE	30 Je ne suis pas aussi intelligent que mon père, mais je suis plus fort que lui.	29 Je ne suis pas aussi fort que mon frère, mais je suis plus beau que lui.	28 Mon frère est plus petit que moi, mais il est plus fort.	27 Mes parents sont moins sympas que mes grands-parents.	26 Mes parents sont plus travailleurs que mes grands-parents.	25 Mon oncle est moins sympa que ma tante.	24 Il est moins affectueux qu'elle.

UNIT 9 – STAIRCASE TRANSLATION

Hi. My name is Charles. I am 12. I have a brother and sister.

Hi. My name is Charles. I am 12. I have a brother and sister. My sister is taller and slimmer than me…

Hi. My name is Charles. I am 12. I have a brother and sister. My sister is taller and slimmer than me, but she is less fun and less hard-working.

Hi. My name is Charles. I am 12. I have a brother and sister. My sister is taller and slimmer than me, but she is less fun and less hard-working. My brother is shorter and fatter than me, but he is also more intelligent, sportier and stronger than me.

Hi. My name is Charles. I am 12. I have a brother and sister. My sister is taller and slimmer than me, but she is less fun and less hard-working. My brother is shorter and fatter than me, but he is also more intelligent, sportier and stronger than me. I have a girlfriend. She is more talkative and funnier than me.

* Hi. My name is Charles. I am 12. I have a brother and sister. My sister is taller and slimmer than me, but she is less fun and less hard-working. My brother is shorter and fatter than me, but he is also more intelligent, sportier and stronger than me. I have a girlfriend. She is more talkative and funnier than me. My best friend, Paul, is as tall and slim as me, but he is a lot stronger. He is very nice.

* Translate the last step here:

⏱ UNIT 9 – FASTER! 🪁

Say:

1. I am taller than my brother.
2. I am less strong than my cousin (f).
3. My sister is less fun than me.
4. My father is shorter than my mother.
5. My grandfather is older than my grandmother.
6. My father is less talkative than my mother.
7. My sister is noisier than my dog.
8. I am more hard-working than my friends.
9. My dog is less intelligent than my cat.
10. My brothers are less handsome than me.

	Time	Mistakes	Referee's name
1			
2			
3			
4			

UNIT 9 – TRAPDOOR

| Je
Il
Elle
Mon frère
Ma sœur
Mon père
Ma mère
Mes parents | est

sont

suis | aussi

moins

plus | amusant(e)(s)
bavard(e)(s)
bruyant(e)(s)
fort(e)(s)
jeune(s)
paresseux/euse(s)
sérieux/euse(s)
sportif/ive(s)
travailleur/euse(s)
vieux/vieille(s) | que | moi.
ma cousine.
mon cousin.
mon frère.
ma sœur.
ma grand-mère.
mon grand-père.
mes grands-parents.
ma tante.
mon oncle. |

1. I (m) am as strong as my cousin (m).
2. I (f) am more hard-working than my brother.
3. My mother is more talkative than my aunt.
4. My father is more serious than my grandfather.
5. My sister is sportier than me.
6. My parents are younger than my grandparents.
7. My sister is older than me.
8. I (m) am older than my cousin (f).
9. My brother is noisier than my sister.
10. My mother is lazier than my grandmother.

UNIT 9 – COMMUNICATIVE DRILLS

1	2	3
Do you have many things in common with your parents, Paul? - Yes, I think so. I am as talkative as my mother and as hard-working as my father. **And how are you different?** - I am slimmer and better looking.	**Do you have many things in common with your father, Serge?** - Yes. I think so. I am as tall and strong as him. **And how are you different?** - I am less fat because I am sportier and less lazy than him.	**Do you have many things in common with your mother, Marie?** - Yes. I think so. I am as good-looking and as relaxed as her. **And how are you different?** - I am a bit fatter and not as tall as her.
4	5	6
Do you have many things in common with your brother, Philippe? - Yes. I think so. I am as talkative, friendly and affectionate as he. **And how are you different?** - I am less lazy and silly.	**Do you have many things in common with your sister, Alexandre?** - No, I don't think so. I am less hard-working, less intelligent and less sporty than her. **And do you have many things in common with your brother?** - Yes. I am as lazy, funny and calm as him.	**Do you have many things in common with your mother, Caroline?** - Yes. I think so. I am as short and slim as her. Also, I am as talkative and affectionate as her. **And how are you different?** - I am a bit less strong and less hard-working than her.

UNIT 9 – COMMUNICATIVE DRILLS REFEREE CARD

1	2	3
Tu as beaucoup de choses en commun avec tes parents, Paul? - Oui. Je pense que oui. Je suis aussi bavard que ma mère et aussi travailleur que mon père. **Et quelles différences as-tu avec eux?** - Je suis plus mince et plus beau.	**Tu as beaucoup de choses en commun avec ton père, Serge?** - Oui. Je pense que oui. Je suis aussi grand et fort que lui. **Et quelles différences as-tu avec lui?** - Je suis moins gros parce que je suis plus sportif et moins paresseux que lui.	**Tu as beaucoup de choses en commun avec ta mère, Marie?** - Oui. Je pense que oui. Je suis aussi belle et aussi tranquille qu'elle. **Et quelles différences as-tu avec elle?** - Je suis un peu plus grosse et pas aussi grande qu'elle.

4	5	6
Tu as beaucoup de choses en commun avec ton frère, Philippe? - Oui. Je pense que oui. Je suis aussi bavard, sympa et affectueux que lui. **Et quelles différences as-tu avec lui?** - Je suis moins paresseux et stupide.	**Tu as beaucoup de choses en commun avec ta sœur, Alexandre?** - Non. Je ne pense pas. Je suis moins travailleur, moins intelligent et moins sportif qu'elle. **Et tu as beaucoup de choses en commun avec ton frère?** - Oui, je suis aussi paresseux, amusant et tranquille que lui.	**Tu as beaucoup de choses en commun avec ta mère, Caroline?** - Oui. Je pense que oui. Je suis aussi petite et mince qu'elle. De plus, je suis aussi bavarde et affectueuse qu'elle. **Et quelles différences as-tu avec elle?** - Je suis un peu moins forte et moins travailleuse qu'elle.

UNIT 9 – SURVEY

	What is your name?	How old are you?	Do you have brothers or sisters?	How are you different from your brother/sister?	How are you similar to your brother/sister?
	Comment tu t'appelles?	**Quel âge as-tu?**	**Tu as des frères ou des sœurs?**	**Quelles différences as-tu avec ton frère / ta sœur?**	**Quelles similarités as-tu avec ton frère / ta sœur?**
e.g.	*Je m'appelle Philippe.*	*J'ai onze ans.*	*J'ai une sœur qui s'appelle Pauline.*	*Je suis plus grand et plus gros que ma sœur. Je suis aussi plus travailleur qu'elle.*	*Je suis aussi beau et sympa qu'elle.*
1.					
2.					
3.					
4.					
5.					
6.					
7.					

UNIT 9 – ANSWERS

FIND SOMEONE WHO

	Find someone whose...	Name
1.	...sister is sportier than their brother.	Rosanne
2.	...sister is more talkative than their brother.	Romain
3.	...brother is nicer than their sister.	Isabelle
4.	...dog is more boring than their cat.	Fernand
5.	...sister is as strong as their brother.	Victor
6.	...sister is more relaxed than their brother.	Martin
7.	...cat is fatter than their dog.	Hélène
8.	...sister is less noisy than their brother.	Sonia
9.	...cat is uglier than their dog.	Serge
10.	...younger brother is shorter than their older brother.	Paul
11.	...sister is as hard-working as their brother.	Léa
12.	...sister is nicer than their brother.	Raphaël
13.	...brother is lazier than a sloth.	Julien
14.	...dog is noisier than their cat.	Patricia
15.	...dog is as stupid as their cat.	Marie
16.	...sister is shorter than their brother.	Oscar

STAIRCASE TRANSLATION

Salut. Je m'appelle Charles. J'ai douze ans. J'ai un frère et une sœur. Ma sœur est plus grande et plus mince que moi, mais elle est moins amusante et moins travailleuse. Mon frère est plus petit et plus gros que moi, mais il est aussi plus intelligent, plus sportif et plus fort que moi. J'ai une petite amie. Elle est plus bavarde et plus amusante que moi. Mon meilleur ami, Paul, est aussi grand et mince que moi, mais il est beaucoup plus fort. Il est très sympa.

FASTER!

REFEREE SOLUTION:

1. Je suis plus grand que mon frère.
2. Je suis moins fort(e) que ma cousine.
3. Ma sœur est moins amusante que moi.
4. Mon père est plus petit que ma mère.
5. Mon grand-père est plus vieux que ma grand-mère.
6. Mon père est moins bavard que ma mère.
7. Ma sœur est plus bruyante que mon chien.
8. Je suis plus travailleur/euse que mes amis.
9. Mon chien est moins intelligent que mon chat.
10. Mes frères sont moins beaux que moi.

TRAPDOOR

1. Je suis plus fort que mon cousin.
2. Je suis plus travailleuse que mon frère.
3. Ma mère est plus bavarde que ma tante.
4. Mon père est plus sérieux que mon grand-père.
5. Ma sœur est plus sportive que moi.
6. Mes parents sont plus jeunes que mes grands-parents.
7. Ma sœur est plus vieille que moi.
8. Je suis plus vieux que ma cousine.
9. Mon frère est plus bruyant que ma sœur.
10. Ma mère est plus paresseuse que ma grand-mère.

Unit 10
Describing my teachers &
saying why I like them

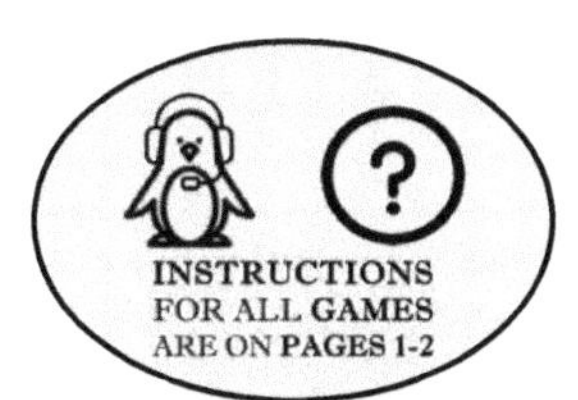

Quel(le) professeur(e) tu (n') aimes (pas)? Pourquoi? — *Which teacher do you (not) like? Why?*
Tu aimes ton/ta professeur(e) de dessin? Pourquoi? — *Do you like your art teacher? Why?*

J'adore *I love* **J'aime** *I like* **Je n'aime pas** *I don't like*	**mon professeur**	**d'**	allemand anglais éducation physique espagnol histoire informatique	**parce qu' il/elle est** *because he/she is*
	ma professeure	**de**	dessin français mathématiques musique sciences technologie théâtre	**parce qu' il/elle n' est pas** *because he/she is not*

Adjectives (masculine):

ennuyeux	*boring*
gentil	*kind*
impatient	*impatient*
intelligent	*intelligent*
intéressant	*interesting*
méchant	*mean*
patient	*patient*
strict	*strict*
travailleur	*hard-working*
drôle	*funny*
sympathique	*nice*

Adjectives (feminine):

ennuyeuse
gentille
impatiente
intéressante
méchante
patiente
stricte
travailleuse

De plus, *Furthermore*	**je l'aime bien** *I like him/her* **je ne l'aime pas** *I don't like him/her*	**car**	**il/elle est toujours** *he/she is always* **il/elle n'est jamais** *he/she is never*	**de bonne humeur** — *in a good mood* **de mauvaise humeur** — *in a bad mood* **en colère** — *angry*
			il/elle *he/she*	**m'aide** — *helps me* **m'écoute** — *listens to me* **me comprend** — *understands me* **me crie dessus** — *shouts at me* **me gronde** — *tells me off* **nous donne peu/trop de devoirs** — *gives us little/too much homework*

UNIT 10 – FIND SOMEONE WHO – Student Cards

Mon professeur de français est sympathique. **ALAIN**	Mon professeur d'espagnol est méchant. **GABRIEL**	Ma professeure de géographie est très stricte. **VALÉRIE**	Ma professeure de géographie m'aide toujours. **SERGE**
Mon professeur de dessin est drôle. **YVAN**	Ma professeure de dessin est intelligente. **STÉPHANE**	Ma professeure d'espagnol est patiente. **VÉRONIQUE**	Ma professeure de français n'est pas stricte. **SYLVIE**
Ma professeure de sciences est très gentille. **ANTHONY**	Ma professeure de sciences est très intéressante. **ANDRÉA**	Ma professeure d'histoire est impatiente. **OLIVIA**	Ma professeure d'histoire ne me gronde jamais. **MARTINE**
Mon professeur d'allemand est travailleur. **ALEXANDRA**	Ma professeur de français est travailleuse. **MYRIAM**	Ma professeure d'espagnol est drôle. **MATHIEU**	Ma professeure d'histoire est ennuyeuse. **AMBRE**

UNIT 10 – FIND SOMEONE WHO – Student Grid

Find someone who...		Name
1.	...has a French teacher who is not strict.	
2.	...has a very kind science teacher.	
3.	...has a very interesting science teacher.	
4.	...has an impatient history teacher.	
5.	...has a history teacher who never tells them off.	
6.	...has a hard-working German teacher.	
7.	...has a hard-working French teacher.	
8.	...has a nice French teacher.	
9.	...has a mean Spanish teacher.	
10.	...has a very strict geography teacher.	
11.	...has a geography teacher who always helps him.	
12.	...has a funny art teacher.	
13.	...has an intelligent art teacher.	
14.	...has a patient Spanish teacher.	
15.	...has a funny Spanish teacher.	
16.	...has a boring history teacher.	

UNIT 10 – ORAL PING PONG – Person A

ENGLISH 1	FRENCH 1	ENGLISH 2	FRENCH 2
I like my German teacher.	J'aime mon/ma professeur(e) d'allemand.	I like my French teacher because he is funny and he listens to me.	J'aime mon professeur de français car il est drôle et il m'écoute.
I love my history teacher.		I don't like my Spanish teacher because he always tells me off.	
I don't like my English teacher.	Je n'aime pas mon/ma professeur(e) d'anglais.	I like my German teacher because he never shouts at me.	J'aime mon professeur d'allemand car il ne me crie jamais dessus.
I love my music teacher.		I don't like my history teacher because he never helps me.	
I like my French teacher.	J'aime mon/ma professeur(e) de français.	I like my English teacher because she is funny and gives us little homework.	J'aime ma professeure d'anglais car elle est drôle et nous donne peu de devoirs.
I like my physics teacher because he is funny.		I don't like my maths teacher because he is boring and always gets angry.	
I don't like my science teacher because she is strict.	Je n'aime pas ma professeure de sciences car elle est stricte.	I like my PE teacher because he is always in a good mood.	J'aime mon professeur d'éducation physique car il est toujours de bonne humeur.
I don't like my maths teacher because he is mean.		I don't like my science teacher because she is mean and gives us a lot of homework.	
I like my drama teacher because she is nice.	J'aime ma professeure de théâtre parce qu'elle est sympathique.	I don't like my art teacher because she never helps me.	Je n'aime pas ma professeure de dessin car elle ne m'aide jamais.
I don't like my technology teacher because he is lazy.		I love my music teacher because he is hard working and funny.	

UNIT 10 – ORAL PING PONG – Person B

ENGLISH 1	FRENCH 1	ENGLISH 2	FRENCH 2
I like my German teacher.		I like my French teacher because he is funny and he listens to me.	
I love my history teacher.	J'adore mon/ma professeur(e) d'histoire.	I don't like my Spanish teacher because he always tells me off.	Je n'aime pas mon professeur d'espagnol car il me gronde toujours.
I don't like my English teacher.		I like my German teacher because he never shouts at me.	
I love my music teacher.	J'adore mon/ma professeur(e) de musique.	I don't like my history teacher because he never helps me.	Je n'aime pas mon professeur d'histoire parce qu'il ne m'aide jamais.
I like my French teacher.		I like my English teacher because she is funny and gives us Little homework.	
I like my physics teacher because he is funny.	J'aime mon professeur de physique parce qu'il est drôle.	I don't like my maths teacher because he is boring and he always gets angry.	Je n'aime pas mon professeur de maths car il est ennuyeux et il est toujours en colère.
I don't like my science teacher because she is strict.		I like my PE teacher because he is always in a good mood.	
I dont' like my maths teacher because he is mean.	Je n'aime pas mon professeur de maths car il est méchant.	I don't like my science teacher because she is mean and gives us a lot of homework.	Je n'aime pas ma professeure de sciences car elle est méchante et nous donne beaucoup de devoirs.
I like my drama teacher because she is nice.		I don't like my art teacher because she never helps me.	
I don't like my technology teacher because he is lazy.	Je n'aime pas mon professeur de technologie car il est paresseux.	I love my music teacher because he is hard-working and funny.	J'adore mon professeur de musique parce qu'il est travailleur et drôle.

No Snakes No Ladders

START	1 I like my science teacher (M).	2 Do you like your maths teacher (M)?	3 I like my Spanish teacher (M) a lot.	4 I don't like my maths teacher (M).	5 I love my art teacher (M).	6 I don't like my English teacher (M).
7 Do you like your French teacher (M)? Why	8 I don't like my science teacher (M).	9 I like my music teacher because she is kind.	10 I like my Spanish teacher because she is very kind.	11 I don't like my drama teacher because he is mean.	12 I love my art teacher because she is interesting and kind.	13 Do you like your science teacher (M)?
14 I don't like my Spanish teacher because she never helps me.	15 I like my English teacher because she is always in a good mood.	16 I don't like my maths teacher because she is mean and strict.	17 I like my history teacher because she understands me.	18 I like my science teacher because she listens to me.	19 Do you like your English teacher (M)?	20 Do you like your drama teacher (M)? Why
21 I love my PE teacher (M) because he never shouts at me.	22 Do you like your science teacher (M)? Why?	23 Do you like your English teacher (M)? Why?	24 My French teacher (M) is always in a good mood.	25 My German teacher (F) always helps me.	26 My music teacher (M) gives us little homework.	27 My maths teacher (F) gives us too much homework.
28 My technology teacher (F) is funny and is never angry.	29 My history teacher (M) always tells me off.	30 My drama teacher (M) always listens to me.	FINISH			

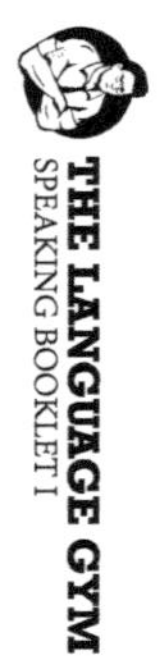

No Snakes No Ladders

DÉPART

1. J'aime mon professeur de sciences.
2. Tu aimes ton professeur de maths?
3. J'aime beaucoup mon professeur d'espagnol.
4. Je n'aime pas mon professeur de maths.
5. J'aime mon professeur de dessin.
6. Je n'aime pas mon professeur d'anglais.
7. Tu aimes ton professeur de français? Pourquoi ?
8. Je n'aime pas mon professeur de sciences.
9. J'aime ma professeure de musique car elle est gentille.
10. J'aime ma professeure d'espagnol car elle est très gentille.
11. Je n'aime pas mon professeur de théâtre car il est méchant.
12. J'aime ma professeure de dessin car elle est intéressante et gentille.
13. Tu aimes ton professeur de sciences?
14. Je n'aime pas ma professeure d'espagnol car elle ne m'aide jamais.
15. J'aime ma professeure d'anglais car elle est toujours de bonne humeur.
16. Je n'aime pas ma professeure de maths car elle est méchante et stricte.
17. J'aime ma professeure d'histoire car elle me comprend.
18. J'aime ma professeure de sciences car elle m'écoute.
19. Tu aimes ton professeur d'anglais?
20. Tu aimes ton professeur de théâtre? Pourquoi?
21. J'adore mon professeur d'éducation physique car il ne me crie jamais dessus.
22. Tu aimes ton professeur de sciences? Pourquoi?
23. Tu aimes ton professeur d'anglais? Pourquoi?
24. Mon professeur de français est toujours de bonne humeur.
25. Ma professeure d'allemand m'aide toujours.
26. Mon professeur de musique nous donne peu de devoirs.
27. Ma professeure de maths nous donne trop de devoirs.
28. Ma professeure de technologie est drôle et n'est jamais en colère.
29. Mon professeur d'histoire me gronde toujours.
30. Mon professeur de théâtre m'écoute toujours.

ARRIVÉE

UNIT 10 – STAIRCASE TRANSLATION

I like my English teacher a lot.

I like my English teacher a lot because she is kind, funny and hard-working.

I like my English teacher a lot because she is kind, funny and hard-working. Moreover, she always listens to me and helps me and...

I like my English teacher a lot because she is kind, funny and hard-working. Moreover, she always listens to me, helps me and understands me.

I like my English teacher a lot because she is kind, funny and hard-working. Moreover, she always listens to me, helps me and understands me. However, I don't like my science teacher.

* I like my English teacher a lot because she is kind, funny and hard-working. Moreover, she always listens to me, helps me and understands me. However, I don't like my science teacher because she is very strict and always tells me off. Moreover, she gives us too much homework.

* Translate the
last step here:

⏱ UNIT 10 – FASTER! 💨

Say:

1. I like my science teacher because she is funny.
2. I like my maths teacher because he is interesting.
3. I like my French teacher because she is always in a good mood.
4. I like my history teacher because she is very kind and interesting.
5. I don't like my Spanish teacher because he never helps me.
6. I don't like my English teacher because he doesn't understand me.
7. I love my music teacher because he never gives us a lot of homework.
8. I don't like my technology teacher because he is boring and mean.

	Time	Mistakes	Referee's name
1			
2			
3			
4			

UNIT 10 – THINGS IN COMMON

	1	2	3	4
Quel est le mois de ton anniversaire?				
Tu as combien de frères et sœurs?				
Comment est ton père?				
Comment est ta mère?				
Quelle est ta matière préférée?				
Que fais-tu pendant ton temps libre?				
Quel est ton sport préféré?				

UNIT 10 – COMMUNICATIVE DRILLS

1	2	3
Do you like your science teacher? Why? - I like my science teacher because he is nice and fun and he always helps me. **Why don't you like your maths teacher?** - I don't like my maths teacher because he is strict and he is never in a good mood.	**Do you like your maths teacher? Why?** - I like my science teacher because he is kind, patient and always listens to me. **Why don't you like your physics teacher?** - I don't like my physics teacher because she is boring, impatient and mean. Moreover, she never helps me when I don't understand.	**Do you like your French teacher? Why?** - I like my French teacher because she is very kind, patient and interesting. Moreover, she is always in a good mood and never shouts at me. **Why don't you like your art teacher?** - I don't like my art teacher because he always tells me off and gives us too much homework.
4	5	6
Do you like your PE teacher? Why? - I like my PE teacher because he is funny and hard-working. Moreover, he gives us little homework. **Why don't you like your science teacher?** - I don't like my science teacher because he doesn't understand me and he always shouts at me.	**Do you like your history teacher? Why?** - I like my history teacher because she is nice and funny. Moreover, she always listens to me and understands me **Why don't you like your music teacher?** - I don't like my music teacher because he is mean and impatient. Moreover, he is always angry and gives us too much homework.	**Do you like your drama teacher? Why?** - I like my drama teacher because she is fun and hard-working. Moreover, she never shouts at me and gives us little homework **Why don't you like your English teacher?** - I don't like my English teacher because she always shouts at me and never helps me. Moreover, she is boring and not very hard-working.

UNIT 10 – COMMUNICATIVE DRILLS
REFEREE CARD

1	2	3
Tu aimes ton professeur de sciences? Pourquoi? - J'aime mon professeur de sciences car il est sympathique et drôle et il m'aide toujours. **Pourquoi tu n'aimes pas ton professeur de mathématiques?** - Je n'aime pas mon professeur de mathématiques car il est strict et il n'est jamais de bonne humeur.	**Tu aimes ton professeur de mathématiques? Pourquoi?** - J'aime mon professeur de mathématiques car il est gentil, patient et m'écoute toujours. **Pourquoi tu n'aimes pas ta professeure de physique?** - Je n'aime pas ma professeure de physique car elle est ennuyeuse, impatiente et méchante. De plus, elle ne m'aide jamais quand je ne comprends pas.	**Tu aimes ta professeure de français? Pourquoi?** - J'aime ma professeure de français car elle est très gentille, patiente et intéressante. De plus, elle est toujours de bonne humeur et elle ne me crie jamais dessus. **Pourquoi tu n'aimes pas ton professeur de dessin?** - Je n'aime pas mon professeur de dessin car il me gronde toujours et nous donne trop de devoirs.

4	5	6
Tu aimes ton professeur d'éducation physique? Pourquoi? - J'aime mon professeur d'éducation physique car il est drôle et travailleur. De plus, il nous donne peu de devoirs. **Pourquoi tu n'aimes pas ton professeur de sciences?** - Je n'aime pas mon professeur de sciences car il ne me comprend pas et il me crie toujours dessus.	**Tu aimes ta professeure d'histoire? Pourquoi?** - J'aime ma professeure d'histoire car elle est sympathique et drôle. De plus, elle m'écoute toujours et me comprend. **Pourquoi tu n'aimes pas ton professeur de musique?** - Je n'aime pas mon professeur de musique car il est méchant et impatient. De plus, il est toujours en colère et nous donne trop de devoirs.	**Tu aimes ta professeure de théâtre? Pourquoi?** - J'aime ma professeure de théâtre car elle est drôle et travailleuse. De plus, elle ne me gronde jamais et nous donne peu de devoirs **Pourquoi tu n'aimes pas ta professeure d'anglais?** - Je n'aime pas ma professeure d'anglais car elle me crie toujours dessus et ne m'aide jamais. De plus, elle est ennuyeuse et pas très travailleuse.

UNIT 10 – SURVEY

	What is your name?	Do you like your maths teacher? Why?	Do you like your English teacher? Why?	Do you like your science teacher? Why?	Do you like your French teacher? Why?
	Comment tu t'appelles?	Tu aimes ton/ta prof de maths? Pourquoi?	Tu aimes ton/ta prof d'anglais? Pourquoi?	Tu aimes ton/ta prof de sciences? Pourquoi?	Tu aimes ton/ta prof de français? Pourquoi?
e.g.	*Je m'appelle Matéo.*	*Non, je n'aime pas mon/ma prof de maths car il/elle nous donne trop de devoirs.*	*Oui j'adore mon/ma prof d'anglais car il/elle m'aide toujours.*	*Oui, j'aime beaucoup mon/ma prof de sciences car il/elle n'est jamais en colère.*	*J'adore mon/ma prof de français car il/elle est toujours de bonne humeur.*
1.					
2.					
3.					
4.					
5.					
6.					
7.					

UNIT 10 – ANSWERS

FIND SOMEONE WHO

Find someone who …		Name
1.	…has a French teacher who is not strict.	Sylvie
2.	…has a very kind science teacher.	Anthony
3.	…has a very interesting science teacher.	Andréa
4.	…has an impatient history teacher.	Olivia
5.	…has a history teacher who never tells them off.	Martine
6.	…has a hard-working German teacher.	Alexandra
7.	…has a hard-working French teacher.	Myriam
8.	…has a nice French teacher.	Alain
9.	…has a mean Spanish teacher.	Gabriel
10.	…has a very strict geography teacher.	Valérie
11.	…has a geography teacher who always helps him.	Serge
12.	…has a funny art teacher.	Yvan
13.	…has an intelligent art teacher.	Stéphane
14.	…has a patient Spanish teacher.	Véronique
15.	…has a funny Spanish teacher.	Mathieu
16.	…has a boring history teacher.	Ambre

STAIRCASE TRANSLATION

J'aime beaucoup ma professeure d'anglais parce qu'elle est gentille, drôle et travailleuse. De plus, elle m'écoute toujours, m'aide et me comprend. Cependant, je n'aime pas ma professeure de sciences parce qu'elle est très stricte et me gronde toujours. De plus, elle nous donne trop de devoirs.

FASTER!

REFEREE SOLUTION:
1. J'aime ma professeure de sciences parce qu'elle est drôle.
2. J'aime mon professeur de mathématiques car il est intéressant.
3. J'aime ma professeure de français parce qu'elle est toujours de bonne humeur.
4. J'aime ma professeure d'histoire car elle est très gentille et intéressante.
5. Je n'aime pas mon professeur d'espagnol car il ne m'aide jamais.
6. Je n'aime pas mon professeur d'anglais car il ne me comprend pas.
7. J'adore mon professeur de musique parce qu'il ne donne jamais de devoirs.
8. Je n'aime pas mon professeur de technologie car il est ennuyeux et méchant.

THINGS IN COMMON

Students give their own answers to the questions and make a note of which students they have things in common with.

UNIT 11
Saying what I and others do in our free time

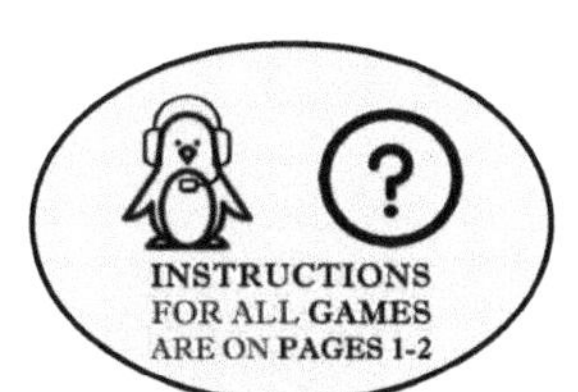

Que fais-tu pendant ton temps libre?	*What do you do in your free time?*
Que fait ton ami(e) pendant son temps libre?	*What does your friend do in his/her free time?*
Quels sports fais-tu?	*What sports do you do?*
Fais-tu d'autres activités?	*Do you do another activities?*
Combien de fois par semaine fais-tu du sport?	*How many times a week do you do sport?*

Je joue *I play* **Il/elle joue** *He/she plays* **Mon ami(e) joue** *My friend plays*	**au basket** *basketball* **au foot** *football* **au tennis** *tennis* **aux cartes** *cards* **aux échecs** *chess* **avec des ami(e)s** *with some friends*	**de temps en temps** *from time to time* **deux fois par semaine** *twice a week*
Je fais *I do* **Il/Elle fait** *He/she does* **Mon ami(e) fait** *My friend does*	**du footing** *jogging* **du ski** *skiing* **du sport** *sport* **du vélo** *cycling* **de l'équitation** *horse riding* **de l'escalade** *rock climbing* **de la natation** *swimming* **de la randonnée** *hiking*	**pendant le week-end** *during the weekend* **tous les jours** *every day* **tous les samedis** *every Saturday*
Je vais *I go* **Il/Elle va** *He/she goes* **Mon ami(e) va** *My friend goes*	**au centre commercial** *to the mall* **au centre sportif** *to the sports centre* **au gymnase** *to the gym* **au parc** *to the park* **à la campagne** *to the countryside* **à la montagne** *to the mountain* **à la pêche** *fishing* **à la piscine** *to the pool* **à la plage** *to the beach* **chez des amis** *to my friends' house -plural* **en boîte** *clubbing*	**tous les soirs** *every evening* **tous les week-ends** *every weekend* **une fois par mois** *once a month*

UNIT 11 – FIND SOMEONE WHO – Student Cards

Pendant mon temps libre, je joue aux cartes. **MATÉO**	Pendant mon temps libre, je fais de l'équitation. **RAPHAËL**	Pendant mon temps libre, je joue aux échecs. **SOPHIE**	Pendant mon temps libre, je joue aux jeux vidéo. **MARIE**
Pendant mon temps libre, je joue au foot. **SYLVAIN**	Pendant mon temps libre, je joue au tennis. **ANDRÉ**	Pendant mon temps libre, je joue au basket. **VALENTINE**	Pendant mon temps libre, je vais au parc. **PIERRE**
Pendant mon temps libre, je fais du vélo. **LÉONARD**	Pendant mon temps libre, je fais de l'escalade. **RACHEL**	Pendant mon temps libre, je vais au gymnase. **LUCIE**	Pendant mon temps libre, je vais à la pêche. **PAUL**
Pendant mon temps libre, je fais du footing. **SÉBASTIEN**	Pendant mon temps libre, je vais chez des amis. **LORÈNE**	Pendant mon temps libre, je fais de la natation. **MARTINE**	Pendant mon temps libre, je vais au centre sportif. **SERGE**

UNIT 11 – FIND SOMEONE WHO – Student Grid

Find someone who...	**Name**
Que fais-tu pendant ton temps libre? *What do you do in your free time?*	
1. ...goes to the gym.	
2. ...goes fishing.	
3. ...goes jogging.	
4. ...goes to a friends' house.	
5. ...plays football.	
6. ...plays tennis.	
7. ...plays basketball.	
8. ...goes to the park.	
9. ...does cycling.	
10. ...does climbing.	
11. ...plays cards.	
12. ...goes horse riding.	
13. ...plays chess.	
14. ...plays videogames.	
15. ...does swimming.	
16. ...goes to the sports centre.	

UNIT 11 – ORAL PING PONG – Person A

ENGLISH 1	FRENCH 1	ENGLISH 2	FRENCH 2
I play chess twice a week.	Je joue aux échecs deux fois par semaine.	**I play cards once a month.**	Je joue aux cartes une fois par mois.
I play tennis from time to time.		**I do horse riding once a week.**	
I go to my friends' house every day.	Je vais chez mes amis tous les jours.	**I do swimming every day.**	Je fais de la natation tous les jours.
I go to the beach every weekend.		**My friend does jogging once a week.**	
I play with my friends every Saturday.	Je joue avec mes amis tous les samedis.	**I do cycling during the weekend.**	Je fais du vélo pendant le week-end.
I go to the mountain once a month.		**I play tennis twice a week.**	
I play basketball from time to time.	Je joue au basket de temps en temps.	**My friend goes clubbing every Saturday.**	Mon ami(e) va en boîte tous les samedis.
I go to the swimming pool every evening.		**I go fishing every evening.**	
I do jogging every day.	Je fais du footing tous les jours.	**I go to the gym twice a week.**	Je vais au gymnase deux fois par semaine.
I do rock climbing twice a week.		**I go to the countryside every weekend.**	

UNIT 11 – ORAL PING PONG – Person B

ENGLISH 1	FRENCH 1	ENGLISH 2	FRENCH 2
I play chess twice a week.		I play cards once a month.	
I play tennis from time to time.	Je joue au tennis de temps en temps.	I do horse riding once a week.	Je fais de l'équitation une fois par semaine.
I go to my friends' house every day.		I do swimming every day.	
I go to the beach every weekend.	Je vais à la plage tous les week-ends.	My friend does jogging once a week.	Mon ami(e) fait du footing une fois par semaine.
I play with my friends every day.		I do cycling during the weekend.	
I go to the mountain once a month.	Je vais à la montagne une fois par mois.	I play tennis twice a week.	Je joue au tennis deux fois par semaine.
I play basketball from time to time.		My friend goes clubbing every Saturday.	
I go to the swimming pool every evening.	Je vais à la piscine tous les soirs.	I go fishing every evening.	Je vais à la pêche tous les soirs.
I do jogging every day.		I go to the gym twice a week.	
I do rock climbing twice a week.	Je fais de l'escalade deux fois par semaine.	I go to the countryside every weekend.	Je vais à la campagne tous les week-ends.

No Snakes No Ladders

START	**1** What do you do in your free time?	**2** I play cards once a month.	**3** I play football every day.	**4** I DO rock climbing twice a week.	**5** What sports do you do?	**6** I DO hiking every weekend.	**7** I DO swimming twice a week.
15 My friend goes clubbing every Saturday.	**14** My friend goes to the gym every day.	**13** My friend DOES ski from time to time.	**12** How many times a week do you play tennis?	**11** I go to the countryside once a month.	**10** My brother DOES rock climbing every Saturday.	**9** My friend DOES horse riding every weekend.	**8** What does your brother do in his free time?
16 My sister goes to the gym every evening.	**17** My father goes to the sports centre twice a week.	**18** My mother plays cards three times a week.	**19** My brother plays tennis every day. I play football every evening.	**20** My brother plays basketball twice a week.	**21** How many times a week do you play football?	**22** What do you do in your free time? How many times a week?	**23** My friend goes to the beach every weekend.
FINISH	**30** In my free time I do sport and I go to the park or to the shopping centre.	**29** In my free time I go to the gym and to the swimming pool.	**28** My older brother goes clubbing every Saturday.	**27** How many times a week do you do sport?	**26** My sister is very sporty. In her free time she DOES ski and cycling.	**25** I do sport once a month. My brother does sport every day.	**24** My friend DOES jogging every day.

No Snakes No Ladders

DÉPART	1 Que fais-tu pendant ton temps libre?	2 Je joue aux cartes une fois par mois.	3 Je joue au foot tous les jours.	4 Je fais de l'escalade deux fois par semaine.	5 Quels sports fais-tu?	6 Je fais de la randonnée tous les week-ends.	7 Je fais de la natation deux fois par semaine.
15 Mon ami(e) va en boîte tous les samedis.	14 Mon ami(e) va au gymnase tous les jours.	13 Mon ami(e) fait du ski de temps en temps.	12 Combien de fois par semaine joues-tu au tennis?	11 Je vais à la campagne une fois par mois.	10 Mon frère fait de l'escalade tous les samedis.	9 Mon ami(e) fait de l'équitation tous les week-ends.	8 Que fait ton frère pendant son temps libre?
16 Ma sœur va au gymnase tous les soirs.	17 Mon père va au centre sportif deux fois par semaine.	18 Ma mère joue aux cartes trois fois par semaine.	19 Mon frère joue au tennis tous les jours. Je joue au foot tous les soirs.	20 Mon frère joue au basket deux fois par semaine.	21 Combien de fois par semaine joues-tu au foot?	22 Que fais-tu pendant ton temps libre? Combien de fois par semaine?	23 Mon ami(e) va à la plage tous les week-ends.
ARRIVÉE	30 Pendant mon temps libre, je fais du sport et je vais au parc ou au centre commercial.	29 Pendant mon temps libre, je vais au gymnase et à la piscine.	28 Mon frère aîné va en boîte tous les samedis.	27 Combien de fois par semaine fais-tu du sport?	26 Ma sœur est très sportive. Pendant son temps libre elle fait du ski et du vélo.	25 Je fais du sport une fois par mois. Mon frère fait du sport tous les jours.	24 Mon ami(e) fait du footing tous les jours.

UNIT 11 – STAIRCASE TRANSLATION

My name is Thomas. I am German.

My name is Thomas. I am German. In my free time I do a lot of sport.

My name is Thomas. I am German. In my free time I do a lot of sport. My favourite sport is rock climbing. I do rock climbing every day.

My name is Thomas. I am German. In my free time I do a lot of sport. My favourite sport is rock climbing. I do rock climbing every day. When the weather is bad I play chess or cards.

My name is Thomas. I am German. In my free time I do a lot of sport. My favourite sport is rock climbing. I do rock climbing every day. When the weather is bad I play chess or cards. I also like to play videogames or Playstation.

* My name is Thomas. I am German. In my free time I do a lot of sport. My favourite sport is rock climbing. I do rock climbing every day. When the weather is bad I play chess or cards. I also like to play videogames or Playstation. I often play PlayStation with my best friend, Karl. Karl plays videogames every evening.

* Translate the
last step here:

⏱ UNIT 11 – FASTER! 🐦

Say:

1. In my free time I often do swimming.
2. I go to the swimming pool three times a week.
3. I also go to the gym twice a week.
4. From time to time I go to the park.
5. I go cycling once a month, but I often go jogging.
6. My brother always plays Playstation.
7. He does sport once a month.
8. My sister often does sport.
9. She plays basketball and tennis.
10. She also goes rock climbing.

	Time	Mistakes	Referee's name
1			
2			
3			
4			

UNIT 11 – FLUENCY CARDS

At the weekend		
On Sunday		
On Friday		
Next weekend		
Tomorrow		
On Sunday		
On Saturday		
At the weekend		

	Time	Mistakes
1		
2		
3		
4		

UNIT 11 – COMMUNICATIVE DRILLS

1	2	3
What do you do in your free time? - I play basketball every day. I also play video games with my friends every day. From time to time I go to the swimming pool with my sister. Once a week, I go to my best friend's (m) house.	**What do you do in your free time?** - I play chess with my brother every day. I also do a lot of sport: I play football every day with my friends and I go jogging in the park three times a week. From time to time, I go to the gym with my brother.	**What do you do in your free time?** - I play on the computer every day. I also like to ride bike ride with my friends. From time to time I play cards. I also go to the shopping mall with my friends every day after school.
4	**5**	**6**
Do you like to play chess? - Yes, I play chess every day. It is interesting. **Do you like to do sport?** - No. I don't like to do sport. It's healthy but very tiring. **Do you like to go fishing?** - Yes, I love it. It is very fun.	**Do you like to play videogames?** - Yes, I play videogames often. It is great! **Do you like to go cycling?** - No, I don't like to do sport. It's very tiring. **Do you go to the shopping mall often?** - No, I rarely go to the shopping mall. It's boring.	**Do you like to go swimming?** - No, I rarely go swimming. **Do you like to play basketball?** - No, I don't like to play basketball. It's very boring and a bit tiring also. **Do you go the gym?** - No, I don't go to the gym. **What do you like to do in your free time?** - I like to go to the park with my friends.
7	**8**	**9**
Do you like to play Playstation? - Yes, I often play on the Playstation. It is interesting and fun. **Do you go to the sports centre?** - No, I don't go to the sports centre or to the gym. It is too tiring. **What do you like to do in your free time?** - I like to cycle in the park with my friend.	**Do you like to go jogging?** - No. I don't like to go jogging. It is too tiring. **Do you like to play football?** - No. I don't like to play football. It's tiring and boring. **Do you go the swimming pool?** - No, I never go to the swimming pool. **What do you like to do in your free time?** - I like to go to my friend's house and play videogames with him.	**Do you like to play football?** - Yes, I play football every day. It is fun. **Do you like to do skiing?** - No. I don't like to do skiing. It's tiring and dangerous *(dangereux)*. **Do you like to go fishing?** - Yes, I love it. It is very fun. I do it twice a week.

UNIT 11 - COMMUNICATIVE DRILLS
REFEREE CARD

1	2	3
Que fais-tu pendant ton temps libre? - Je joue au basket tous les jours. Je joue aussi aux jeux vidéo avec mes amis tous les jours. De temps en temps je vais à la piscine avec ma sœur. Une fois par semaine, je vais chez mon meilleur ami.	**Que fais-tu pendant ton temps libre?** - Je joue aux échecs avec mon frère tous les jours. Je fais aussi beaucoup de sport: je joue au foot tous les jours avec mes amis et je fais du footing dans le parc trois fois par semaine. De temps en temps, je vais au gymnase avec mon frère.	**Que fais-tu pendant ton temps libre?** - Je joue sur l'ordinateur tous les jours. J'aime aussi faire du vélo avec mes amis. De temps en temps je joue aux cartes. Je vais aussi au centre commercial avec mes amis tous les jours après le collège.

4	5	6
Tu aimes jouer aux échecs? - Oui, je joue aux échecs tous les jours. C'est intéressant. **Tu aimes faire du sport?** - Non. Je n'aime pas faire du sport. C'est sain, mais très fatigant. **Tu aimes aller à la pêche?** - Oui, j'adore cela. C'est très amusant.	**Tu aimes jouer aux jeux vidéo?** - Oui, je joue souvent aux jeux vidéo. C'est génial! **Tu aimes faire du vélo?** - Non, je n'aime pas faire du sport. C'est très fatigant. **Tu vas souvent au centre commercial?** - Non, je vais rarement au centre commercial. C'est ennuyeux.	**Tu aimes faire de la natation?** - Non, je vais rarement faire de la natation. **Tu aimes jouer au basket?** - Non, je n'aime pas jouer au basket. C'est très ennuyeux et un peu fatigant aussi. **Tu vas au gymnase?** - Non, je ne vais pas au gymnase. **Qu'est-ce que tu aimes faire pendant ton temps libre?** - J'aime aller au parc avec mes amis.

7	8	9
Tu aimes jouer à la Playstation? - Oui, je joue souvent à la Playstation. C'est intéressant et amusant. **Tu vas au centre sportif?** - Non, je ne vais pas au centre sportif ou au gymnase. C'est trop fatigant. **Qu'est-ce que t aimes faire pendant ton temps libre?** - J'aime faire du vélo au parc avec mon ami.	**Tu aimes faire du footing?** - Non, je n'aime pas faire du footing. C'est trop fatigant. **Tu aimes jouer au foot?** - Non, je n'aime pas jouer au foot. C'est fatigant et ennuyeux. **Tu vas à la piscine?** - Non, je ne vais jamais à la piscine. **Qu'est-ce que tu aimes faire pendant ton temps libre?** - J'aime aller chez mon ami et jouer aux jeux vidéo avec lui.	**Tu aimes jouer au foot?** - Oui, je joue au foot tous les jours. C'est amusant. **Tu aimes faire du ski?** - Non. Je n'aime pas faire du ski. C'est fatigant et dangereux. **Tu aimes aller à la pêche?** - Oui, j'adore cela. C'est très amusant. Je fais cela deux fois par semaine.

UNIT 11 – SURVEY

	What is your name?	What do you do in your free time? Why do you like it?	How many times a week do you play videogames?	How many times a week do you do sport?	How many times a week do you go to the shopping mall?
	Comment tu t'appelles?	Que fais-tu pendant ton temps libre? Pourquoi tu aimes ça?	Combien de fois par semaine joues-tu aux jeux vidéo?	Combien de fois par semaine fais-tu du sport?	Combien de fois par semaine vas-tu au centre commercial?
e.g.	*Je m'appelle Guillaume.*	*Pendant mon temps libre, je fais de l'équitation. J'aime ça parce que c'est relaxant.*	*Je joue aux jeux vidéo tous les jours.*	*Je fais du sport cinq fois par semaine.*	*Je vais au centre commercial une fois par semaine.*
1.					
2.					
3.					
4.					
5.					
6.					
7.					

UNIT 11 – ANSWERS

FIND SOMEONE WHO

	Find someone who...	Name
1.	...goes to the gym.	Lucie
2.	...goes fishing.	Paul
3.	...goes jogging.	Sébastien
4.	...goes to a friends' house.	Lorène
5.	...plays football.	Sylvain
6.	...plays tennis.	André
7.	...plays basketball.	Valentine
8.	...goes to the park.	Pierre
9.	...does cycling.	Léonard
10.	...does climbing.	Rachel
11.	...plays cards.	Matéo
12.	...goes horse riding.	Raphaël
13.	...plays chess.	Sophie
14.	...plays videogames.	Marie
15.	...does swimming.	Martine
16.	...goes to the sports centre.	Serge

STAIRCASE TRANSLATION

Je m'appelle Thomas. Je suis allemand. Pendant mon temps libre, je fais beaucoup de sport. Mon sport préféré, c'est l'escalade. Je fais de l'escalade tous les jours. Quand il fait mauvais, je joue aux échecs ou aux cartes. J'aime aussi jouer aux jeux vidéo ou à la Playstation. Je joue souvent à la Playstation avec mon meilleur ami, Karl. Karl joue aux jeux vidéo tous les soirs.

FASTER! REFEREE SOLUTION:

1. Pendant mon temps libre, je fais souvent de la natation.
2. Je vais à la piscine trois fois par semaine.
3. Je vais aussi au gymnase deux fois par semaine.
4. De temps en temps, je vais au parc.
5. Je fais du vélo une fois par mois, mais je fais souvent du footing.
6. Mon frère joue toujours à la Playstation.
7. Il fait du sport une fois par mois.
8. Ma sœur fait souvent du sport.
9. Elle joue au basket et au tennis.
10. Elle fait aussi de l'escalade.

FLUENCY CARDS

Pendant le weekend, je vais au cinéma pour regarder un film d'horreur.
Le dimanche, je fais de la natation à la piscine.
Le vendredi, je vais à la plage pour bronzer *(to sunbathe)*.
Le week-end prochain *(next weekend)*, je vais aller au centre commercial pour acheter des vêtements.
Demain, je vais aller au parc pour faire du vélo.
Dimanche, je vais aller au gymnase pour faire de la musculation *(bodybuilding)*.
Le samedi, je vais au stade pour voir un match de foot.
Le week-end, je vais en boîte pour danser.

UNIT 12
Talking about my daily routine

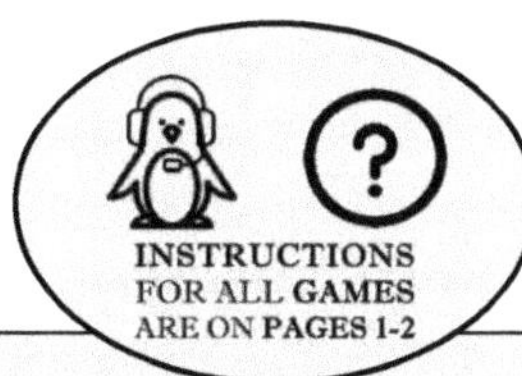

Parle-moi de ta routine journalière. — *Tell me about your daily routine.*
À quelle heure tu te lèves? — *What time do you get up?*
Comment vas-tu au collège? — *How do you go to school?*
Que fais-tu après le collège? — *What do you do after school?*

Vers... *Around...*		**je me brosse les dents** *I brush my teeth*	
À... *At*		**je me coiffe** *I do my hair*	
cinq heures *5*		**je me couche** *I go to bed*	
six heures *6*		**je déjeune** *I have lunch*	
sept heures *7*	**du matin** *in the morning*	**je dîne** *I have dinner*	
huit heures cinq *8.05*		**je fais mes devoirs** *I do my homework*	**ensuite...** *then*
huit heures dix *8.10*		**je m'habille** *I get dressed*	
huit heures et quart *8.15*	**de l'après-midi** *in the afternoon*	**je joue sur l'ordinateur** *I play on the computer*	
huit heures vingt *8.20*			**après...** *after*
huit heures vingt-cinq *8.25*		**je me lève** *I get up*	
huit heures et demie *8.30*		**je prends le petit-déjeuner** *I have breakfast*	
neuf heures moins vingt-cinq *8.35*	**du soir** *in the evening*		**finalement...** *finally*
neuf heures moins vingt *8.40*		**je regarde la télé** *I watch TV*	
neuf heures moins le quart *8.45*		**je rentre à la maison** *I go back home*	
neuf heures moins dix *8.50*		**je me repose** *I rest*	
neuf heures moins cinq *8.55*		**je sors de chez moi** *I leave my house*	
À midi *12pm*		**je vais au collège en bus** *I go to school by bus*	
À minuit *12am*			

UNIT 12 – FIND SOMEONE WHO – Student Cards

Je prends le petit-déjeuner à six heures. Je déjeune à une heure. Je dîne à huit heures. **DENIS**	Je prends le petit-déjeuner à sept heures. Je déjeune à midi. Je dîne à huit heures et demie. **GUILLAUME**	Je prends le petit-déjeuner à huit heures. Je déjeune à deux heures. Je dîne à sept heures. **GÉRALDINE**	Je prends le petit-déjeuner à six heures et demie. Je déjeune à une heure. Je dîne à huit heures. **SERGE**
Je ne prends pas de petit-déjeuner. Je déjeune à une heure moins vingt-cinq. Je dîne à six heures et demie. **CHARLES**	Je prends le petit-déjeuner à six heures et quart. Je déjeune à midi et demie. Je dîne à huit heures vingt-cinq. **PHILIPPE**	Je prends le petit-déjeuner à huit heures moins le quart. Je déjeune à une heure et demie. Je dîne à huit heures et demie. **VICTOIRE**	Je prends le petit-déjeuner à sept heures moins dix. Je ne déjeune pas. Je dîne à huit heures cinq. **ANNA**
Je prends le petit-déjeuner à cinq heures et demie. Je déjeune à midi vingt. Je dîne à sept heures et demie. **PATRICIA**	Je prends le petit-déjeuner à sept heures moins cinq. Je déjeune à midi. Je ne dîne pas. **JULIE**	Je prends le petit-déjeuner à sept heures moins dix. Je déjeune à midi cinq. Je dîne à neuf heures moins le quart. **MICHEL**	Je prends le petit-déjeuner à huit heures et demie. Je déjeune à une heure moins cinq. Je dîne à neuf heures. **PAUL**
Je prends le petit-déjeuner à six heures et demie. Je déjeune à midi et demie. Je dîne à huit heures. **JOËL**	Je ne prends pas de petit-déjeuner. Je déjeune à une heure moins le quart. Je dîne à huit heures. **AURORE**	Je prends le petit-déjeuner à sept heures. Je déjeune à une heure et quart. Je dîne à huit heures cinq. **CATHERINE**	Je prends le petit-déjeuner à six heures. Je déjeune à une heure vingt-cinq. Je dîne à huit heures. **JULIEN**

UNIT 12 – FIND SOMEONE WHO – Student Grid

	Find someone who...	Name
1.	...has breakfast at 6:00.	
2.	...has lunch at 12:00.	
3.	...has dinner at 7:00.	
4.	...has lunch at 1:00.	
5.	...doesn't have breakfast.	
6.	...has lunch at 12:30.	
7.	...has dinner at 8:30.	
8.	...doesn't have lunch.	
9.	...has breakfast at 5:30.	
10.	...doesn't have dinner.	
11.	...has breakfast at 6:50.	
12.	...has dinner at 9:00.	
13.	...has lunch at 1.15.	

UNIT 12 – ORAL PING PONG – Person A

ENGLISH 1	FRENCH 1	ENGLISH 2	FRENCH 2
I get up at 6:00.	Je me lève à six heures.	I rest.	Je me repose.
I shower at 6:15.		I do my homework.	
I get dressed at 6:30.	Je m'habille à six heures et demie.	I go to the sports centre.	Je vais au centre sportif.
I have breakfast at 7:45.		I play football.	
I brush my teeth at 7:00.	Je me brosse les dents à sept heures.	I play videogames.	Je joue aux jeux vidéo.
I leave my house at 7:15.		I play chess.	
I go to school by bus at 7:00.	Je vais au collège en bus à sept heures.	I go on a bike ride.	Je fais du vélo.
I have lunch at 12:30.		I watch television.	
I go back home by bus at 3:00.	Je rentre à la maison en bus à trois heures.	I have dinner at eight.	Je dîne à huit heures.
I do my homework.		I go to bed at 11:00.	

UNIT 12 – ORAL PING PONG – Person B

ENGLISH 1	FRENCH 1	ENGLISH 2	FRENCH 2
I get up at 6:00.		I rest.	
I shower at 6:15.	Je me douche à six heures et quart.	I do my homework.	Je fais mes devoirs.
I get dressed at 6:30.		I go to the sports centre.	
I have breakfast at 7:45.	Je prends le petit-déjeuner à huit heures moins le quart.	I play football.	Je joue au foot.
I brush my teeth at 7:00.		I play videogames.	
I leave my house at 7:15.	Je sors de chez moi à sept heures et quart.	I play chess.	Je joue aux échecs.
I go to school by bus at 7:00.		I go on a bike ride.	
I have lunch at 12:30.	Je déjeune à midi et demie.	I watch television.	Je regarde la télé.
I go back home by bus at 3:00.		I have dinner at eight.	
I do my homework.	Je fais mes devoirs.	I go to bed at 11:00.	Je me couche à onze heures.

No Snakes No Ladders

START

1. What time do you get up?
2. Tell me about your daily routine.
3. What do you do in the morning?
4. I get up at seven.
5. I shower.
6. I get dressed.
7. My brother is called Paul
8. I brush my teeth.
9. I have breakfast at 7:45.
10. I leave my house at 8:00.
11. At what time do you go to school?
12. I go to school at 8:15.
13. At what time do you have lunch?
14. I have lunch at 1:00.
15. I leave school at 3:00.
16. I go back home at 4:00.
17. I go back home and then I do my homework.
18. I go back home and after I rest a bit.
19. I shower, I have breakfast and then I brush my teeth.
20. I get up, I shower and after I have breakfast.
21. I get up at 7:30.
22. I go to school by bus.
23. Tell me about your daily routine.
24. I brush my teeth and I leave my house at around 8:15.
25. I go to school by bus at around 8:30.
26. What do you do on a typical day?
27. I have breakfast at 7:45.
28. I have dinner and then I watch television or I play videogames.
29. I have dinner, I brush my teeth, I shower and I go to bed.
30. I have dinner at 7:30 and after, I do my homework.

FINISH

No Snakes No Ladders

DÉPART / 1	2	3	4	5	6	7
1 À quelle heure tu te lèves?	**2** Parle-moi de ta routine journalière.	**3** Que fais-tu le matin?	**4** Je me lève à sept heures.	**5** Je me douche.	**6** Je m'habille.	**7** Mon frère s'appelle Paul.
14 Je déjeune à une heure.	**13** À quelle heure déjeunes-tu?	**12** Je vais au collège à huit heures et quart.	**11** À quelle heure vas-tu au collège?	**10** Je sors de chez moi à huit heures.	**9** Je prends le petit-déjeuner à huit heures moins le quart.	**8** Je me brosse les dents.
15 Je sors du collège à trois heures.	**18** Je rentre à la maison et après je me repose un peu.	**19** Je me douche, je prends le petit-déjeuner et ensuite je me brosse les dents.	**20** Je me lève, je me douche et après je prends le petit-déjeuner.	**21** Je me lève à sept heures et demie.	**22** Je vais au collège en bus.	**23** Parle-moi de ta routine journalière.
16 Je rentre à la maison à quatre heures.	**17** Je rentre à la maison et ensuite je fais mes devoirs.					**24** Je me brosse les dents et je sors de chez moi vers huit heures et quart.
ARRIVÉE	**30** Je dîne à sept heures et demie et après, je fais mes devoirs.	**29** Je dîne, je me brosse les dents, je me douche et je me couche.	**28** Je dîne et ensuite je regarde la télé ou je joue aux jeux vidéo.	**27** Je prends le petit-déjeuner à huit heures moins le quart.	**26** Que fais-tu pendant une journée typique?	**25** Je vais au collège en bus vers huit heures et demie.

UNIT 12 – STAIRCASE TRANSLATION

My name is Caroline. I am 11. Normally, I get up at around 6:15.

My name is Caroline. I am 11. Normally, I get up at around 6:15. Then I shower and I have breakfast with my brother.

My name is Caroline. I am 11. Normally, I get up at around 6:15. Then I shower and have breakfast with my brother. Afterwards, I brush my teeth and I get dressed.

My name is Caroline. I am 11. Normally, I get up at around 6:15. Then I shower and I have breakfast with my brother. Afterwards, I brush my teeth and I get dressed. Then, I prepare my bag.

My name is Caroline. I am 11. Normally, I get up around 6:15. Then I shower and I have breakfast with my brother. Afterwards, I brush my teeth and I get dressed. Then, I prepare my bag. At around 7:30 I leave my house and I go to school by bus. I arrive at school at around 8:00.

* My name is Caroline. I am 11. Normally, I get up at around 6:15. Then I shower and I have breakfast with my brother. Afterwards, I brush my teeth and I get dressed. Then, I prepare my bag. At around 7:30 I leave my house and I go to school by bus. I arrive at school at around 8:00. I return home at 4:00 and then I do my homework.

* Translate the
last step here:

⏱ UNIT 12 – FASTER! 🕊

Say:

1. I get up at 6:15.
2. I shower at 6:25.
3. I have breakfast at 6:30.
4. Then, I brush my teeth.
5. I get dressed around 6:40.
6. I prepare my bag.
7. I leave my house at 6:50.
8. I go to school by bus.
9. I arrive at school at 7:30.
10. I have lunch at 12:40.

	Time	Mistakes	Referee's name
1			
2			
3			
4			

UNIT 12 – FAST & FURIOUS

1. Je me lève à _______________   (6:30 am)

2. Je prends le petit-déjeuner vers _______________   (6:45 am)

3. Je me brosse les dents vers _______________   (7:00 am)

4. Je sors de chez moi à _______________   (7:15 am)

5. J'arrive au collège à _______________   (7:45 am)

6. Je rentre à la maison à _______________   (3:50 pm)

7. Je fais mes devoirs à _______________   (4:00 pm)

8. Je dîne à _______________   (8:15 pm)

9. Je regarde la télé jusqu'à _______________   (10:30 pm)

10. Je me couche à _______________   (11:45 pm)

	Time 1	Time 2	Time 3	Time 4
Time				
Mistakes				

UNIT 12 – COMMUNICATIVE DRILLS

1	2	3
At what time do you get up? - I get up at 6:30. **What do you do after that?** - I have breakfast, I brush my teeth, get dressed, watch a bit of television, then I leave the house.	**At what time do you have dinner?** - I have dinner at around 7:30 in the evening. **What do you do after that?** - I watch television, then I brush my teeth, I shower and finally I go to bed.	**At what time do you eat?** - Normally, I have breakfast early, at around 6 o'clock in the morning. Then, I have lunch at school, at 12:00 and finally I have dinner at around 7:30 in the evening.

4	5	6
At what time do you leave your house? - Normally, I leave my house at 7:45. **At what time do you get back home?** - I get back home at around 4:00. **At what time do you go to bed?** - I go to bed at around 10:45.	**At what time do you get up?** - I get up at 7:15 **What do you do after that?** - I have breakfast, I brush my teeth, get dressed, watch a bit of television, then I leave the house. **At what time do you get back home?** - I get back home at around 4:30.	**At what time do you have dinner?** - I have dinner at around 7:45 in the evening. **What do you do after that?** - I watch television, then I brush my teeth, I shower and finally I go to bed. **At what time do you get up?** - At around 6:00 in the morning.

7	8	9
At what time do you get up? - I usually get up at around 6:30. **At what time do you eat?** - Normally I have breakfast at around seven o'clock in the morning. I have lunch at school, at around 12:30 and have dinner at around 8:00 in the evening.	**At what time do you leave your house?** - Normally, I leave my house at 7:45. **At what time do you get back home?** - At around 4:00. **What time do you go to bed?** - I go to bed at around 10:45.	**At what time do you get up?** - I usually get up at around 7:30. **At what time do you have dinner?** - I have dinner at around 7:00 in the evening. **What do you do after that?** - I watch television, then I brush my teeth, I shower and finally I go to bed.

UNIT 12 - COMMUNICATIVE DRILLS
REFEREE CARD

1	2	3
À quelle heure tu te lèves? - Je me lève à six heures et demie. **Que fais-tu après cela?** - Je prends le petit-déjeuner, je me brosse les dents, je m'habille, je regarde un peu la télé et ensuite je sors de chez moi.	**À quelle heure tu dînes?** - Je dîne vers sept heures et demie du soir. **Que fais-tu après cela?** - Je regarde la télé, ensuite je me brosse les dents, je me douche et finalement je me couche.	**À quelle heure tu manges?** - Normalement, je prends le petit-déjeuner tôt, vers six heures du matin. Ensuite, je déjeune au collège à midi et finalement je dîne vers sept heures et demie du soir.
4	**5**	**6**
À quelle heure tu sors de chez toi? - Normalement, je sors de chez moi à huit heures moins le quart. **À quelle heure tu rentres à la maison?** - Je rentre à la maison vers quatre heures. **À quelle heure tu te couches?** - Je me couche vers onze heures moins le quart.	**À quelle heure tu te lèves?** - Je me lève à sept heures et quart. **Que fais-tu après cela?** - Je prends le petit-déjeuner, je me brosse les dents, je m'habille, je regarde un peu la télé et ensuite je sors de chez moi. **À quelle heure tu rentres à la maison?** - Je rentre à la maison vers quatre heures et demie.	**À quelle heure tu dînes?** - Je dîne à huit heures moins le quart du soir. **Que fais-tu après cela?** - Je regarde la télé, ensuite je me brosse les dents, je me douche et finalement je me couche. **À quelle heure tu te lèves?** - Vers six heures du matin.
7	**8**	**9**
À quelle heure tu te lèves? - Normalement, je me lève vers six heures et demie. **À quelle heure tu prends le petit-déjeuner?** - Normalement, je prends le petit-déjeuner vers sept heures du matin. Je déjeune au collège vers midi et demie et je dîne vers huit heures du soir.	**À quelle heure tu sors de chez toi?** - Normalement, je sors de chez moi à huit heures moins le quart. **À quelle heure tu rentres à la maison?** - Vers quatre heures. **À quelle heure tu te couches?** - Je me couche vers onze heures moins le quart.	**À quelle heure tu te lèves?** - Normalement, je me lève vers sept heures et demie. **À quelle heure tu dînes?** - Je dîne vers sept heures du soir. **Que fais-tu après cela?** - Je regarde la télé, ensuite je me brosse les dents, je me douche et finalement je me couche.

UNIT 12 – SURVEY

	What is your name?	At what time do you get up and go to bed?	At what time do you have breakfast, lunch and dinner?	How do you go to school?	What do you do after dinner?
	Comment tu t'appelles?	À quelle heure tu te lèves et tu te couches?	À quelle heure tu prends le petit-déjeuner, le déjeuner et le dîner?	Comment vas-tu au collège?	Que fais-tu après le dîner?
e.g.	*Je m'appelle Béatrice.*	*Je me lève à six heures du matin et je couche à dix heures du soir.*	*Je prends le petit-déjeuner à sept heures du matin, je déjeune à midi et je dîne vers sept heures du soir.*	*Je vais au collège en bus.*	*Après le dîner, je regarde la télé avec ma famille.*
1.					
2.					
3.					
4.					
5.					
6.					
7.					

UNIT 12 – ANSWERS

FIND SOMEONE WHO

	Find someone who...	Name
1.	...has breakfast at 6:00.	Denis / Julien
2.	...has lunch at 12:00.	Guillaume / Julie
3.	...has dinner at 7:00.	Géraldine
4.	...has lunch at 1:00.	Denis/ Serge
5.	...doesn't have breakfast.	Charles / Aurore
6.	...has lunch at 12:30.	Philippe / Joël
7.	...has dinner at 8:30.	Guillaume / Victoire
8.	...doesn't have lunch.	Anna
9.	...has breakfast at 5:30.	Patricia
10.	...doesn't have dinner.	Julie
11.	...has breakfast at 6:50.	Michel / Anna
12.	...has dinner at 9:00.	Paul
13.	...has lunch at 1.15.	Catherine

STAIRCASE TRANSLATION

Je m'appelle Caroline. J'ai onze ans. Normalement, je me lève vers six heures et quart. Ensuite, je me douche et je prends le petit-déjeuner avec mon frère. Après, je me brosse les dents et je m'habille. Ensuite, je prépare mon sac. Vers sept heures et demie, je sors de chez moi et je vais au collège en bus. J'arrive au collège vers huit heures. Je rentre à la maison à quatre heures et ensuite je fais mes devoirs.

FASTER! REFEREE SOLUTION:

1. Je me lève à six heures et quart.
2. Je me douche à six heures vingt-cinq.
3. Je prends le petit-déjeuner à six heures et demie.
4. Ensuite, je me brosse les dents.
5. Je m'habille vers sept heures moins vingt.
6. Je prépare mon sac.
7. Je sors de chez moi à sept heures moins dix.
8. Je vais au collège en bus.
9. J'arrive au collège à sept heures et demie.
10. Je déjeune à une heure moins vingt.

FAST & FURIOUS

1. Je me lève à **six heures et demie**.
2. Je prends le petit-déjeuner vers **sept heures moins le quart**.
3. Je me brosse les dents vers **sept heures**.
4. Je sors de chez moi à **sept heures et quart**.
5. J'arrive au collège à **huit heures moins le quart**.
6. Je rentre à la maison à **quatre heures moins dix**.
7. Je fais mes devoirs à **quatre heures**.
8. Je dîne à **huit heures et quart**.
9. Je regarde la télé jusqu'à **dix heures et demie**.
10. Je me couche à **minuit moins le quart**.

UNIT 13
Saying where I and others are going to go at the weekend and what we are going to do

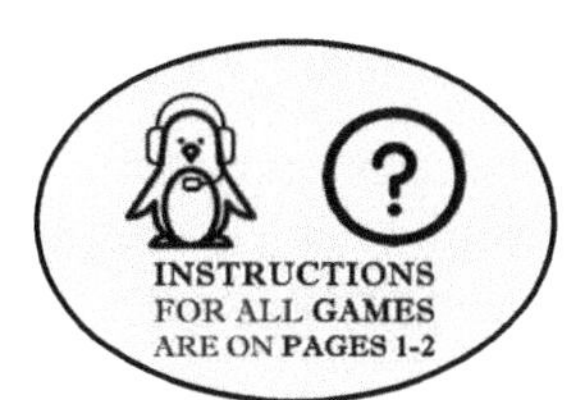

Qu'est-ce que tu vas faire le week-end prochain?	*What are you going to do next weekend?*
Où voudrais-tu aller?	*Where would you like to go?*
Quels sont les projets de ton frère/ta sœur?	*What are your brother/sister's plans?*
Où va aller ton frère/ta sœur?	*Where is your brother/sister going to go?*

Le week-end prochain *Next weekend* Vendredi *On Friday* Samedi *On Saturday*	**je vais aller** *I am going to go* **je voudrais aller** *I would like to go* **ma sœur va aller** *my sister is going to go* **mon ami(e) va aller** *my friend is going to go* **mon frère va aller** *my brother is going to go*	**au**	**centre commercial**	*shopping mall*
			centre sportif	*sports centre*
			cinéma	*cinema*
			gymnase	*gym*
			parc	*park*
			stade	*stadium*
		à la	**pêche**	*fishing*
			piscine	*pool*
			plage	*beach*
		en	**boîte**	*clubbing*
		faire	**les magasins**	*shopping*

je vais aller <u>me</u> promener	*I am going to go for a walk*
il/elle va aller <u>se</u> promener	*he/she is going to go for a walk*

...avec *...with*	**ma (f)** **mon (m)** *my* **sa (f)** **son (m)** *his/her*	**frère** *brother* **meilleure amie** *best friend (f)* **meilleur ami** *best friend (m)* **petite amie** *girlfriend* **petit ami** *boyfriend* **sœur** *sister*	**pour** *(in order) to*	**acheter des choses**	*buy things*
				acheter des vêtements	*buy clothes*
				bronzer	*sunbathe*
				danser	*dance*
				faire de la musculation	*do bodybuilding*
				faire du vélo	*ride my bike*
				jouer au foot	*play football*
				nager	*swim*
				regarder un film	*watch a film*
				regarder/voir un match	*watch/see a match*

Ce sera amusant *It will be fun*	**Ce sera ennuyeux** *It will be boring*	**Ce sera fatigant** *It will be tiring*	**Ce sera relaxant** *It will be relaxing*

UNIT 13 – FIND SOMEONE WHO – Student Cards

Le week-end prochain, je vais aller au centre commercial avec mes amis. **ROMAIN**	Le week-end prochain, je vais aller au cinéma avec ma petite amie. **JEAN**	Le week-end prochain, je vais aller faire les magasins avec ma sœur. **HÉLÈNE**	Le week-end prochain, je vais aller au gymnase avec mes amis. **ANNA**
Le week-end prochain, je vais aller me promener avec ma petite amie. **ÉDOUARD**	Le week-end prochain, je vais aller me promener avec mon petit ami. **AMBRE**	Le week-end prochain, je vais aller au gymnase avec mon frère. **JOANNA**	Le week-end prochain, je vais aller au centre sportif avec mes amis. **PIERRE**
Le week-end prochain, je vais aller au centre commercial avec mes amies. **MARIE**	Le week-end prochain, je vais aller au cinéma avec mon petit ami. **RENÉE**	Le week-end prochain, je vais aller à la pêche avec mes amies. **ISABELLE**	Le week-end prochain, je vais aller au stade avec mes amis. **VICTOR**
Le week-end prochain, je vais aller en boîte avec mes amies. **YOANN**	Le week-end prochain, je vais aller au parc avec mes amis. **CLAIRE**	Le week-end prochain, je vais aller à la piscine avec mes amies. **THÉRÈSE**	Le week-end prochain, je vais aller faire les magasins avec ma sœur. **SUZANNE**

UNIT 13 – FIND SOMEONE WHO – Student Grid

Find someone who...	Name
Qu'est-ce que tu vas faire le week-end prochain? *What are you going to do next weekend?*	
1. ...is going to go to the shopping mall with his friends.	
2. ...is going to go to the cinema with his girlfriend.	
3. ...is going to go to the swimming pool with her female friends.	
4. ...is going to go to the gym with her friends.	
5. ...is going to go for a walk with his girlfriend.	
6. ...is going to go for a walk with her boyfriend.	
7. ...is going to go to the gym with her brother.	
8. ...is going to go to the sports centre with his friends.	
9. ...is going to go to the shopping mall with her friends.	
10. ...is going to go to the cinema with her boyfriend.	
11. ...is going to go fishing with her female friends.	
12. ...is going to go to the stadium with his friends.	
13. ...is going to go clubbing with his female friends.	
14. ...is going to go to the park with her friends.	
15. ...is going to go shopping with their sister.	

UNIT 13 – ORAL PING PONG – Person A

ENGLISH 1	FRENCH 1	ENGLISH 2	FRENCH 2
Next weekend I am going to go to the cinema.	Le week-end prochain, je vais aller au cinéma.	On Friday I am going to go to the gym to do bodybuilding.	Vendredi, je vais aller au gymnase pour faire de la musculation.
On Friday I am going to go fishing.		On Saturday I am going to go to the swimming pool to swim.	
On Saturday I am going to go shopping.	Samedi, je vais aller faire les magasins.	Next weekend I am going to go to the beach to sunbathe.	Le week-end prochain, je vais aller à la plage pour bronzer.
What are you going to do next weekend?		On Friday I am going to go to the park to ride the bike.	
Next weekend I am going to go to the stadium with my friends.	Le week-end prochain, je vais aller au stade avec mes amis.	On Saturday I am going to the stadium to watch a match.	Samedi, je vais aller au stade pour regarder/voir un match.
On Friday I am going to go to the swimming pool with my sister.		Next weekend I am going to the shopping centre to buy clothes.	
On Saturday I am going to go for a walk with my brother.	Samedi, je vais aller me promener avec mon frère.	Next weekend I am going to buy clothes.	Le week-end prochain, je vais acheter des vêtements.
On Saturday I am going to go to the gym with my friends.		On Saturday I am going to the swimming pool. It will be fun.	
On Friday I am going to go to the beach with my best friend (m).	Vendredi, je vais aller à la plage avec mon meilleur ami.	On Friday I am going to go shopping with my mother. It will be boring.	Vendredi, je vais aller faire les magasins avec ma mère. Ce sera ennuyeux.
Next weekend I am going to go fishing with my best (female) friend.		On Saturday I am going to go to the gym with my brother to do weights. It will be tiring.	

UNIT 13 – ORAL PING PONG – Person B

ENGLISH 1	FRENCH 1	ENGLISH 2	FRENCH 2
Next weekend I am going to go to the cinema.		On Friday I am going to go to the gym to do weights.	
On Friday I am going to go fishing.	Vendredi, je vais aller à la pêche.	On Saturday I am going to go to the swimming pool to swim.	Samedi, je vais aller à la piscine pour nager.
On Saturday I am going to go shopping.		Next weekend I am going to go to the beach to sunbathe.	
What are you going to do next weekend?	Qu'est-ce que tu vas faire le week-end prochain?	On Friday I am going to go to the park to ride my bike.	Vendredi, je vais aller au parc pour faire du vélo.
Next weekend I am going to go to the stadium with my friends.		On Saturday I am going to the stadium to watch a match.	
On Friday I am going to go to the swimming pool with my sister.	Vendredi, je vais aller à la piscine avec ma sœur.	Next weekend I am going to the shopping centre to buy clothes.	Le week-end prochain, je vais aller au centre commercial pour acheter des vêtements.
On Saturday I am going to go for a walk with my brother		What are you going to do next weekend?	
On Saturday I am going to go to the gym with my friends.	Samedi, je vais aller au gymnase avec mes amis.	On Saturday I am going to the swimming pool. It will be fun.	Samedi, je vais aller à la piscine. Ce sera amusant.
On Friday I am going to go to the beach with my best friend .		On Friday I am going to go shopping with my mother. It will be boring.	
Next weekend I am going to go fishing with my best (female) friend.	Le week-end prochain, je vais aller à la pêche avec ma meilleure amie.	On Saturday I am going to go to the gym with my brother to do weights. It will be tiring.	Samedi, je vais aller au gymnase avec mon frère pour faire de la musculation. Ce sera fatigant.

No Snakes No Ladders

1 — Next week I am going to go fishing.

2 — On Friday I am going to go shopping.

3 — On Saturday I am going to go to the swimming pool.

4 — What are you going to do next weekend?

5 — Where are you going to go on Friday?

6 — Next Saturday I am going to go to the gym.

7 — Next weekend I am going to go to the beach to sunbathe.

8 — On Saturday I am going to go shopping with my sister.

9 — On Friday I am going to go to the shopping centre with my mother.

10 — On Friday I am going to go to the park with my best friend (M).

11 — Next weekend I am going to go to the stadium.

12 — What are you going to do next weekend?

13 — On Saturday I am going to go clubbing.

14 — On Friday my friend (M) is going to go shopping.

15 — Where are you going to go on Friday?

START

16 — On Friday my brother is going to go to the swimming pool to swim.

17 — On Friday my best friend (M) is going to go to the shopping centre to buy clothes.

18 — On Saturday my brother is going to go for a walk with my sister.

19 — Next weekend I am going to go clubbing to dance.

20 — On Friday my older brother is going to go clubbing.

21 — What are you going to do on Friday?

22 — On Saturday I am going to go to the stadium to watch a match.

23 — Next weekend I am going to go to the cinema to watch a movie.

24 — I am going to play football. It will be tiring but fun.

25 — I am going to ride my bike in the park. It will be fun.

26 — I am going to go for a walk with my brother. It will be relaxing.

27 — Where are you going to go on Saturday?

28 — I am going to go swimming with my friends. It will be fun.

29 — I am going to go to the gym to do bodybuilding.

30 — I am going to go fishing with my father. It will be boring.

FINISH

No Snakes No Ladders

DÉPART	**1** La semaine prochaine, je vais aller à la pêche.	**2** Vendredi, je vais aller faire les magasins.	**3** Samedi, je vais aller à la piscine.	**4** Qu'est-ce que tu vas faire le week-end prochain?	**5** Où vas-tu aller vendredi?	**6** Samedi prochain, je vais aller au gymnase.	**7** Le week-end prochain, je vais aller à la plage pour bronzer.
15 Où vas-tu aller vendredi?	**14** Vendredi, mon ami va aller faire les magasins.	**13** Samedi, je vais aller en boîte.	**12** Qu'est-ce que tu vas faire le week-end prochain?	**11** Le week-end prochain, je vais aller au stade.	**10** Vendredi, je vais aller au parc avec mon meilleur ami.	**9** Vendredi, je vais aller au centre commercial avec ma mère.	**8** Samedi, je vais aller faire les magasins avec ma sœur.
16 Vendredi, mon frère va aller à la piscine pour nager.	**17** Vendredi, mon meilleur ami va aller au centre commercial pour acheter des vêtements.	**18** Samedi, mon frère va aller se promener avec ma sœur.	**19** Le week-end prochain, je vais aller en boîte pour danser.	**20** Vendredi, mon frère aîné va aller en boîte.	**21** Qu'est-ce que tu vas faire vendredi?	**22** Samedi, je vais aller au stade pour voir un match.	**23** Le week-end prochain, je vais aller au cinéma pour regarder un film.
ARRIVÉE	**30** Je vais aller à la pêche avec mon père. Ce sera ennuyeux.	**29** Je vais aller au gymnase pour faire de la musculation.	**28** Je vais aller nager avec mes amis. Ce sera amusant.	**27** Où vas-tu aller samedi?	**26** Je vais aller me promener avec mon frère. Ce sera relaxant.	**25** Je vais faire du vélo au parc. Ce sera amusant.	**24** Je vais jouer au foot. Ce sera fatigant, mais amusant.

UNIT 13 – STAIRCASE TRANSLATION

Next weekend I am going to go to the stadium with my father to watch a football match.

Next weekend I am going to go to the stadium with my father to watch a football match. I am also going to the shopping centre with my mother to buy clothes.

Next weekend I am going to go to the stadium with my father to watch a football match. I am also going to the shopping centre with my mother to buy clothes. Afterwards, I am going to go to the park to ride my bike with my friends.

Next weekend I am going to go to the stadium with my father to watch a football match. I am also going to the shopping centre with my mother to buy clothes. Afterwards, I am going to go to the park to do cycling with my friends. Finally, I am going to go to the cinema with my best ...

Next weekend I am going to go to the stadium with my father to watch a football match. I am also going to the shopping centre with my mother to buy clothes. Afterwards, I am going to go to the park to do cycling with my friends. Finally, I am going to go to the cinema with my best friend to watch an action movie.

* Next weekend I am going to go to the stadium with my father to watch a football match. I am also going to the shopping centre with my mother to buy clothes. Afterwards, I am going to go to the park to do cycling with my friends. Finally, I am going to go to the cinema with my best friend to watch an action movie. It will be fun but tiring.

* Translate the
last step here:

⏱ UNIT 13 – FASTER! 🚀

Say:

1. On Friday I am going to go to the shopping mall to buy clothes.
2. My brother is going to go clubbing with his friends.
3. On Saturday I am going to go to the swimming pool with my parents.
4. My brother is going to go to a party with his girlfriend.
5. On Sunday I am going to go to the gym to do bodybuilding.
6. My brother is going to go to the beach with his best friend (m).
7. I am also going to the cinema with my best friend to watch an action movie.
8. My brother is going to go to the park to ride a bike with his friends.
9. It will be fun.
10. But it will be tiring too.

	Time	Mistakes	Referee's name
1			
2			
3			
4			

UNIT 13 – THINGS IN COMMON

Que préfères-tu?	1	2	3	4	5
Aller au centre commercial ou au parc?					
Jouer au foot ou au basket?					
Faire de la natation ou de l'équitation?					
Regarder une comédie ou un film d'horreur?					
Faire du vélo ou du footing?					
Aller à la plage ou au gymnase?					
Regarder un match de foot au stade ou à la télé?					

UNIT 13 – COMMUNICATIVE DRILLS

1	2	3
What are you going to do next weekend? - On Saturday I am going to go to the swimming pool with my parents to swim. On Sunday I am going to go to the gym to do weights.	**What are you going to do next weekend?** - On Saturday I am going to go to the stadium with my father to watch a football match. On Sunday I am going to go to the sports centre to play basketball.	**What are you going to do next weekend?** - On Saturday I am going to go to the park with my friends to ride my bike. On Sunday I am going to go to the shopping centre to buy clothes.
4	5	6
What are you going to do next weekend? - On Saturday I am going to go to the cinema with my friends to watch a movie. On Sunday I am going to go to the beach with my girlfriend to sunbathe. It will be relaxing.	**What are you going to do next weekend?** - On Saturday I am going to go for a walk with my girlfriend. It will be relaxing. On Sunday I am going to go to the sports centre to play football with my friends. It will be fun but tiring.	**What are you going to do next weekend?** - On Saturday I am going to go to a party with my friends to dance and have fun *(m'amuser)*. On Sunday I am going to go to the sports centre to play tennis with my girlfriend. It will be fun.
7	8	9
What are you going to do next weekend? - On Saturday I am going to go to the stadium with my friends to watch a rugby match. On Sunday I am going to go to the sports centre to play basketball. It will be fun.	**What are you going to do next weekend?** - On Saturday I am going to go fishing with my father and my brother. It will be boring. On Sunday I am going to go shopping with my best friend (f). It will be interesting.	**What are you going to do next weekend?** - On Saturday I am going to go for a walk with my boyfriend. It will be relaxing. On Sunday I am going to go to the sports centre to play basketball with my friends. It will be fun but tiring.

UNIT 13 – COMMUNICATIVE DRILLS REFEREE CARD

1	2	3
Qu'est-ce que tu vas faire le week-end prochain? - Samedi, je vais aller à la piscine avec mes parents pour nager. Dimanche, je vais aller au gymnase pour faire de la musculation.	**Qu'est-ce que tu vas faire le week-end prochain?** - Samedi, je vais aller au stade avec mon père pour voir un match de foot. Dimanche, je vais aller au centre sportif pour jouer au basket.	**Qu'est-ce que tu vas faire le week-end prochain?** - Samedi, je vais aller au parc avec mes amis pour faire du vélo. Dimanche, je vais aller au centre commercial pour acheter des vêtements.
4	**5**	**6**
Qu'est-ce que tu vas faire le week-end prochain? - Samedi, je vais aller au cinéma pour regarder un film. Dimanche, je vais aller à la plage avec ma petite amie pour bronzer. Ce sera relaxant.	**Qu'est-ce que tu vas faire le week-end prochain?** - Samedi, je vais aller me promener avec ma petite amie. Ce sera relaxant. Dimanche, je vais aller au centre sportif pour jouer au foot avec mes amis. Ce sera amusant, mais fatigant.	**Qu'est-ce que tu vas faire le week-end prochain?** - Samedi, je vais aller à une fête avec mes amis pour danser et m'amuser. Dimanche, je vais aller au centre sportif pour jouer au tennis avec ma petite amie. Ce sera amusant.
7	**8**	**9**
Qu'est-ce que tu vas faire le week-end prochain? - Samedi, je vais aller au stade avec mes amis pour voir un match de rugby. Dimanche, je vais aller au centre sportif pour jouer au basket. Ce sera amusant.	**Qu'est-ce que tu vas faire le week-end prochain?** - Samedi, je vais aller à la pêche avec mon père et mon frère. Ce sera ennuyeux. Dimanche, je vais aller faire les magasins avec ma meilleure amie. Ce sera intéressant.	**Qu'est-ce que tu vas faire le week-end prochain?** - Samedi, je vais aller me promener avec mon petit ami. Ce sera relaxant. Dimanche, je vais aller au centre sportif pour jouer au basket avec mes amis. Ce sera amusant, mais fatigant.

UNIT 13 – SURVEY

	What is your name?	What do you like to do in your free time?	What are you going to do on Friday after school? With whom?	What are you going to do on Saturday? With whom?	What are you going to do on Sunday? With whom?	And your brother? What is he going to do next weekend?
	Comment tu t'appelles	Qu'est-ce que tu aimes faire pendant ton temps libre?	Qu'est-ce que tu vas faire vendredi après le collège? Avec qui?	Qu'est-ce que tu vas faire samedi? Avec qui?	Qu'est-ce que tu vas faire dimanche? Avec qui?	Et ton frère? Qu'est-ce qu'il va faire le week-end prochain?
e.g.	*Je m'appelle Michel.*	*J'aime jouer à la Playstation et au foot avec mes amis.*	*Vendredi, après le collège, je vais aller au centre sportif pour jouer au basket avec mon frère.*	*Samedi, je vais aller faire les magasins avec ma mère.*	*Dimanche, je vais aller au parc avec ma petite amie.*	*Le week-end prochain, mon frère va aller au restaurant italien avec sa petite amie pour dîner.*
1.						
2.						
3.						
4.						
5.						
6.						

UNIT 13 – ANSWERS

FIND SOMEONE WHO

	Find someone who...	Name
1.	...is going to go to the shopping mall with his friends.	Romain
2.	...is going to go to the cinema with his girlfriend.	Jean
3.	...is going to go to the swimming pool with her female friends.	Thérèse
4.	...is going to go to the gym with her friends.	Anna
5.	...is going to go for a walk with his girlfriend.	Édouard
6.	...is going to go for a walk with her boyfriend.	Ambre
7.	...is going to go to the gym with her brother.	Joanna
8.	...is going to go to the sports centre with his friends.	Pierre
9.	...is going to go to the shopping mall with her friends.	Marie
10.	...is going to go to the cinema with her boyfriend.	Renée
11.	...is going to go fishing with her female friends.	Isabelle
12.	...is going to go to the stadium with his friends.	Victor
13.	...is going to go clubbing with his female friends.	Yoann
14.	...is going to go to the park with her friends.	Claire
15.	...is going to go shopping with their sister.	Hélène / Suzanne

STAIRCASE TRANSLATION

Le week-end prochain, je vais aller au stade avec mon père pour regarder/voir un match de foot. Je vais aussi aller au centre commercial avec ma mère pour acheter des vêtements. Après, je vais aller au parc pour faire du vélo avec mes amis. Finalement, je vais aller au cinéma avec mon/ma meilleur(e) ami(e) pour regarder un film d'action. Ce sera amusant, mais fatigant.

FASTER!

REFEREE SOLUTION:

1. Vendredi, je vais aller au centre commercial pour acheter des vêtements.
2. Mon frère va aller en boîte avec ses amis.
3. Samedi, je vais aller à la piscine avec mes parents.
4. Mon frère va aller à une fête avec sa petite amie.
5. Dimanche, je vais aller au gymnase pour faire de la musculation.
6. Mon frère va aller à la plage avec son meilleur ami.
7. Je vais aussi aller au cinéma avec mon meilleur ami pour regarder un film d'action.
8. Mon frère va aller au parc pour faire du vélo avec ses amis.
9. Ce sera amusant.
10. Mais ce sera aussi fatigant.

THINGS IN COMMON

Students give their own answers to the questions and make a note of which students they have things in common with.

UNIT 14
Talking about food

Qu'est-ce que tu aimes manger et boire? Pourquoi? *What do you like to eat and drink? Why*

J'adore *I love*	**le café**	*coffee*		**dégoûtant**	*disgusting*
	le chocolat	*chocolate*		**délicieux**	*delicious*
	le fromage	*cheese*		**dur**	*hard*
	le jus de fruits	*fruit juice*		**épicé**	*spicy*
J'aime **beaucoup** *I like a lot*	**le lait**	*milk*	***parce que c'est** *because it is*	**gras**	*greasy*
	le miel	*honey*		**juteux**	*juicy*
	le pain	*bread*		**malsain**	*unhealthy*
	le poisson	*fish*		**rafraîchissant**	*refreshing*
J'aime *I like*	**le poulet rôti**	*roast chicken*		**sain**	*healthy*
	le riz	*rice*		**savoureux**	*tasty*
	la salade verte	*green salad*		**sucré**	*sweet*
J'aime un peu *I like a bit*	**la viande**	*meat*			
	l'eau *water* (l' + vowel)				
Je n'aime pas *I don't like*	**les chocolats** *chocolates*			**dégoûtant(e)s**	
	les fruits	*fruit*	**parce qu'ils sont** *because they are*	**délicieux/euses**	
	les hamburgers *burgers*			**dur(e)s**	
	les légumes	*vegetables*		**épicé(e)s**	
	les œufs	*eggs*		**gras(se)s**	
Je déteste *I hate*	**les bananes**	*bananas*		**juteux/euses**	
	les fraises	*strawberries*		**malsain(e)s**	
	les crevettes	*prawns*	****parce qu'elles sont** *because they are*	**rafraîchissant(e)s**	
Je préfère *I prefer*	**les oranges**	*oranges*		**sain(e)s**	
	les pommes	*apples*		**savoureux/euses**	
	les tomates	*tomatoes*		**sucré(e)s**	

PLEASE NOTE
* After "c'est" an adjective is always in its masculine singular form
E.g. J'aime la viande, c'est délicieux.
** However, in the second section after "ils sont" or "elles sont", adjectives agree both in gender and number
E.g. J'aime les œufs parce qu'ils sont sains.
E.g. J'aime les tomates parce qu'elles sont saines.

UNIT 14 – FIND SOMEONE WHO – Student Cards

J'aime le poisson. Je n'aime pas la viande. **LÉONARD**	J'aime le riz. Je n'aime pas le fromage. **RAPHAËL**	J'aime les légumes. Je n'aime pas le poulet. **DIANE**	J'aime la viande. Je n'aime pas le poisson. **PAUL**
J'aime les chocolats. Je n'aime pas les légumes. **SÉBASTIEN**	J'aime les bananes. Je n'aime pas les pommes. **ANDRÉ**	J'aime les hamburgers. Je n'aime pas les saucisses. **DANIELA**	J'aime les crevettes. Je n'aime pas le riz. **ALEXANDRA**
J'aime les crevettes. Je n'aime pas les oranges. **DANIEL**	J'aime les tomates. Je n'aime pas les champignons. **ALEXANDRE**	J'aime le poisson. Je n'aime pas les hamburgers. **OLIVIA**	J'aime les œufs. Je n'aime pas les fraises. **JULES**
J'aime les tomates. Je n'aime pas les cerises. **LUCAS**	J'aime les oranges. Je n'aime pas les épinards. **VALÉRIE**	J'aime le poulet. Je n'aime pas les épinards. **MYRIAM**	J'aime les œufs. Je n'aime pas le poisson. **ÉRIC**

UNIT 14 – FIND SOMEONE WHO – Student Grid

Find someone who...		**Name**
1.	...doesn't like meat.	
2.	...likes rice.	
3.	...likes vegetables.	
4.	...likes meat.	
5.	...likes chocolates.	
6.	...likes bananas.	
7.	...doesn't like sausages.	
8.	...likes prawns.	
9.	...doesn't like oranges.	
10.	...likes tomatoes.	
11.	...likes fish.	
12.	...doesn't like chicken.	
13.	...likes eggs.	
14.	...doesn't like spinach.	

UNIT 14 – ORAL PING PONG – Person A

ENGLISH 1	FRENCH 1	ENGLISH 2	FRENCH 2
I love bread.	J'adore le pain.	I love meat because it is rich in protein.	J'adore la viande car c'est riche en protéines.
I like cheese.		I like chicken a lot because it is healthy.	
I prefer water.	Je préfère l'eau.	I love coffee because it is delicious.	J'adore le café parce que c'est délicieux.
I like fruit a lot.		I hate eggs because they are disgusting.	
I hate meat.	Je déteste la viande.	I don't like hamburgers because they are greasy.	Je n'aime pas les hamburgers parce qu'ils sont gras.
I love chocolate.		I don't like cheese because it is salty.	
I like bananas a lot.	J'aime beaucoup les bananes.	I love fruits because they are delicious.	J'adore les fruits parce qu'ils sont délicieux.
I love tomatoes.		I hate fish because it is disgusting.	
I don't like fish.	Je n'aime pas le poisson.	I don't like carrots because they are hard.	Je n'aime pas les carottes parce qu'elles sont dures.
I like green salad because it is refreshing.		I love apples because they are healthy and delicious.	

UNIT 14 – ORAL PING PONG – Person B

ENGLISH 1	FRENCH 1	ENGLISH 2	FRENCH 2
I love bread.		I love meat because it is rich in protein.	
I like cheese.	J'aime le fromage.	I like chicken a lot because it is healthy.	J'aime le poulet parce que c'est sain.
I prefer water.		I love coffee because it is delicious.	
I like fruit a lot.	J'aime beaucoup les fruits.	I hate eggs because they are disgusting.	Je déteste les œufs parce qu'ils sont dégoûtants.
I hate meat.		I don't like hamburgers because they are greasy.	
I love chocolate.	J'adore le chocolat.	I don't like cheese because it is salty.	Je n'aime pas le fromage car c'est salé.
I like bananas a lot.		I love fruits because they are delicious.	
I love tomatoes.	J'adore les tomates.	I hate fish because it is disgusting.	Je déteste le poisson car c'est dégoûtant.
I don't like fish.		I don't like carrots because they are hard.	
I like green salad because it is refreshing.	J'aime la salade verte parce que c'est rafraîchissant.	I love apples because they are healthy and delicious.	J'adore les pommes car elles sont saines et délicieuses.

No Snakes No Ladders

START

1. Do you like fish? Why?
2. Do you like meat? Why?
3. Do you prefer meat or fish?
4. I prefer chicken because it is healthy.
5. I don't like carrots because they are hard.
6. I love eggs because they are healthy and rich in protein.
7. I don't like vegetables because they are disgusting.
8. I like roast chicken because it is delicious.
9. I like cheese a lot because it is salty.
10. I love fruit juice because it is healthy and refreshing.
11. Do you prefer apples or bananas?
12. I love hamburgers but they are not very healthy.
13. I love honey because it is sweet.
14. I love rice because it is healthy.
15. I don't like milk because it is disgusting.
16. I love vegetables because they are healthy.
17. I don't like hamburgers because they are greasy.
18. Do you prefer bread or rice?
19. Do you prefer tomatoes or carrots?
20. I hate tomatoes because they are disgusting.
21. I love fish because it is tasty and healthy.
22. I don't like honey because it is too sweet.
23. I don't like crevettes because they are disgusting.
24. I love fruits because they are healthy and delicious.
25. I don't like chocolates because they are sweet.
26. I love bananas because they are healthy and delicious.
27. I love milk because it is rich in protein.
28. I love chocolates because they are sweet.
29. I don't like cheese because it is greasy.
30. I love tomatoes because thet are healthy and refreshing.

FINISH

No Snakes No Ladders

DÉPART

1 — Tu aimes le poisson? Pourquoi?

2 — Tu aimes la viande? Pourquoi?

3 — Tu préfères la viande ou le poisson?

4 — Je préfère le poulet parce que c'est sain.

5 — Je n'aime pas les carottes car elles sont dures.

6 — J'adore les œufs car ils sont sains et riches en protéines.

7 — Je n'aime pas les légumes car ils sont dégoûtants.

8 — J'aime le poulet rôti car c'est délicieux.

9 — J'aime beaucoup le fromage car c'est salé.

10 — J'adore le jus de fruits car c'est sain et rafraîchissant.

11 — Tu préfères les pommes ou les bananes?

12 — J'adore les hamburgers mais ils ne sont pas très sains.

13 — J'adore le miel parce que c'est sucré.

14 — J'adore le riz car c'est sain.

15 — Je n'aime pas le lait parce que c'est dégoûtant.

16 — J'adore les légumes parce qu'ils sont sains.

17 — Je n'aime pas les hamburgers parce qu'ils sont gras.

18 — Tu préfères le pain ou le riz?

19 — Tu préfères les tomates ou les carottes?

20 — Je déteste les tomates car elles sont dégoûtantes.

21 — J'adore le poisson car c'est savoureux et sain.

22 — Je n'aime pas le miel car c'est trop sucré.

23 — Je n'aime pas les crevettes parce qu'elles sont dégoûtantes.

24 — J'adore les fruits car ils sont sains et délicieux.

25 — Je n'aime pas les chocolats car ils sont sucrés.

26 — J'adore les bananes car elles sont saines et délicieuses.

27 — J'adore le lait car c'est riche en protéines.

28 — J'adore les chocolats parce qu'ils sont sucrés.

29 — Je n'aime pas le fromage car c'est gras.

30 — J'adore les tomates car elles sont saines et rafraîchissantes.

ARRIVÉE

UNIT 14 – STAIRCASE TRANSLATION

What do I like to eat?

What do I like to eat? I love roast chicken because it is healthy and delicious.

What do I like to eat? I love roast chicken because it is healthy and delicious. I also love vegetables because they are rich in vitamins and minerals.

What do I like to eat? I love roast chicken because it is healthy and delicious. I also love vegetables because they are rich in vitamins and minerals. I also like cheese very much because it is salty and tasty.

What do I like to eat? I love roast chicken because it is healthy and delicious. I also love vegetables because they are rich in vitamins and minerals. I also like cheese very much because it is salty and tasty. Moreover, I like tomatoes because they are refreshing and very healthy.

* What do I like to eat? I love roast chicken because it is healthy and delicious. I also love vegetables because they are rich in vitamins and minerals. I also like cheese very much because it is salty and tasty. Moreover, I like tomatoes because they are refreshing and very healthy. I hate fish. It is healthy, but it is disgusting! And you? What do you like?

* Translate the
last step here:

"""

⏱ UNIT 14 – FASTER! 🕊

Say:

1. I love roast chicken…
2. …because it is tasty and healthy.
3. I like tomatoes a lot…
4. …because they are refreshing and delicious.
5. I like meat a lot too…
6. …because it is rich in protein.
7. I hate hamburgers…
8. …because they are greasy and disgusting.
9. I don't like chocolate…
10. …because it is too sweet and it is not healthy.

	Time	Mistakes	Referee's name
1			
2			
3			
4			

UNIT 14 – THINGS IN COMMON

Qu'est-ce que tu préfères?	1	2	3	4	5
La viande ou les légumes?					
Les carottes ou les tomates?					
Le café ou le thé?					
Le jus d'orange ou le jus de pomme?					
La salade ou les hamburgers					
La glace au chocolat ou la glace à la fraise?					
Le pain ou le riz?					

UNIT 14 – COMMUNICATIVE DRILLS

1	2	3
Do you prefer meat or fish? - I prefer meat because it is rich in protein and it is delicious. **Do you like vegetables?** - No, I don't like vegetables because they are disgusting.	**What do you like to eat?** - I love bread and rice. I also like roast chicken. It is delicious. **What do you not like to eat?** - I hate eggs. They are disgusting.	**What do you not like to eat?** - I don't like vegetables, eggs and burgers. **Why?** - I don't like vegetables because they are disgusting. I don't like eggs because they are not healthy and I don't like burgers because they are greasy.

4	5	6
Do you like roast chicken? - Yes, I love roast chicken. It's tasty and healthy. **Do you like vegetables?** - Vegetables are healthy but I don't like them. They are disgusting.	**Do you like eggs?** - Yes, I love eggs because they are delicious and rich in protein. **Do you like tomatoes?** - No, I don't like them. Tomatoes are healthy but they are disgusting.	**Do you like hamburgers?** - Yes, I like hamburgers because they are tasty. But they are greasy and not healthy. **Do you like roast chicken?** - Yes, I love roast chicken because it is tasty and rich in protein.

7	8	9
Do you like chocolates? - Yes, I love chocolates because they are sweet and delicious. **Do you like honey?** I also *(aussi)* love honey, especially *(surtout)* with bread. It is sweet, delicious and healthy.	**What do you love to eat?** - I love vegetables. They are healthy and delicious. I also love seafood *(fruits de mer)*, especially *(surtout)* prawns because they are tasty and healthy. **What do you hate to eat?** - I hate hamburgers because they are greasy and quite unhealthy.	**What do you like to eat?** - I like green salad with tomatoes because it is refreshing and tasty. **What do you not like to eat?** - I don't like meat because it is greasy and it is not healthy. I don't like milk. It is disgusting.

1	2	3
Tu préfères la viande ou le poisson? - Je préfère la viande parce que c'est riche en protéines et c'est délicieux. **Tu aimes les légumes?** - Non, je n'aime pas les légumes parce qu'ils sont dégoûtants.	**Qu'est-ce que tu aimes manger?** - J'adore le pain et le riz. J'aime aussi le poulet rôti. C'est délicieux. **Qu'est-ce que tu n'aimes pas manger?** - Je déteste les œufs. Ils sont dégoûtants.	**Qu'est-ce que tu n'aimes pas manger?** - Je n'aime pas les légumes, les œufs et les hamburgers. **Pourquoi?** - Je n'aime pas les légumes car ils sont dégoûtants. Je n'aime pas les œufs parce qu'ils ne sont pas sains et je n'aime pas les hamburgers car ils sont gras.
4	**5**	**6**
Tu aimes le poulet rôti? - Oui, j'aime le poulet rôti. C'est savoureux et sain **Tu aimes les légumes?** - Les légumes sont sains, mais je ne les aime pas. Ils sont dégoûtants.	**Tu aimes les œufs?** - Oui, j'adore les œufs car ils sont délicieux et riches en protéines. **Tu aimes les tomates?** - Non, je ne les aime pas. Les tomates sont saines, mais elles sont dégoûtantes.	**Tu aimes les hamburgers?** - Oui j'aime les hamburgers parce qu'ils sont savoureux. Mais ils sont gras et ils ne sont pas sains. **Tu aimes le poulet rôti?** - Oui, j'adore le poulet rôti parce que c'est savoureux et riche en protéines.
7	**8**	**9**
Tu aimes les chocolats? - Oui, j'adore les chocolats parce qu'ils sont sucrés et délicieux. **Tu aimes le miel?** - J'adore aussi le miel, surtout avec du pain. C'est sucré, délicieux et sain.	**Qu'est-ce que tu adores manger?** - J'adore les légumes. Ils sont sains et délicieux. J'aime aussi les fruits de mer, surtout les crevettes parce qu'elles sont savoureuses et saines. **Qu'est-ce que tu détestes manger?** - Je déteste les hamburgers parce qu'ils sont gras et assez malsains.	**Qu'est-ce que tu aimes manger?** - J'aime la salade verte avec des tomates car c'est rafraîchissant et savoureux. **Qu'est-ce que tu n'aimes pas manger?** - Je n'aime pas la viande car c'est gras et ce n'est pas sain. Je n'aime pas le lait. C'est dégoûtant.

UNIT 14 – SURVEY

	What is your name?	What do you like to eat?	What don't you like to eat?	What do you like to drink?	What don't you like to drink?
	Comment tu t'appelles?	Qu'est-ce que tu aimes manger?	Qu'est-ce que tu n'aimes pas manger?	Qu'est-ce que tu aimes boire?	Qu'est-ce que tu n'aimes pas boire?
e.g.	*Je m'appelle Pauline.*	*J'aime manger des œufs car ils sont sains et riches en protéines.*	*Je n'aime pas les hamburgers parce qu'ils sont gras.*	*J'aime beaucoup boire du jus d'orange car c'est rafraîchissant et sain.*	*Je n'aime pas le lait parce c'est dégoûtant.*
1.					
2.					
3.					
4.					
5.					
6.					
7.					

UNIT 14 – ANSWERS

FIND SOMEONE WHO

Find someone who...		Name
1.	...doesn't like meat.	Léonard
2.	...likes rice.	Raphaël
3.	...likes vegetables.	Diane
4.	...likes meat.	Paul
5.	...likes chocolates.	Sébastien
6.	...likes bananas.	André
7.	...doesn't like sausages.	Daniela
8.	...likes prawns.	Alexandra
9.	...doesn't like oranges.	Daniel
10.	...likes tomatoes.	Alexandre / Lucas
11.	...likes fish.	Olivia / Léonard
12.	...doesn't like chicken.	Diane
13.	...likes eggs.	Jules / Éric
14.	...doesn't like spinach.	Valérie / Myriam

STAIRCASE TRANSLATION

Qu'est-ce que j'aime manger? J'adore le poulet rôti parce que c'est sain et délicieux. J'adore aussi les légumes parce qu'ils sont riches en vitamines et minéraux. J'aime aussi beaucoup le fromage parce que c'est salé et savoureux. De plus, j'aime les tomates parce qu'elles sont rafraîchissantes et très saines. Je déteste le poisson. C'est sain, mais c'est dégoûtant! Et toi? Qu'est-ce que tu aimes?

FASTER!

REFEREE SOLUTION:

1. J'adore le poulet rôti...
2. ...parce que c'est savoureux et sain.
3. J'aime beaucoup les tomates...
4. ...parce qu'elles sont rafraîchissantes et délicieuses.
5. J'aime aussi beaucoup la viande...
6. ...parce que c'est riche en protéines.
7. Je déteste les hamburgers...
8. ...parce qu'ils sont gras et dégoûtants.
9. Je n'aime pas le chocolat...
10. ...parce que c'est trop sucré et ce n'est pas sain.

THINGS IN COMMON

Students give their own answers to the questions and make a note of which students they have things in common with.

UNIT 15
My holiday plans

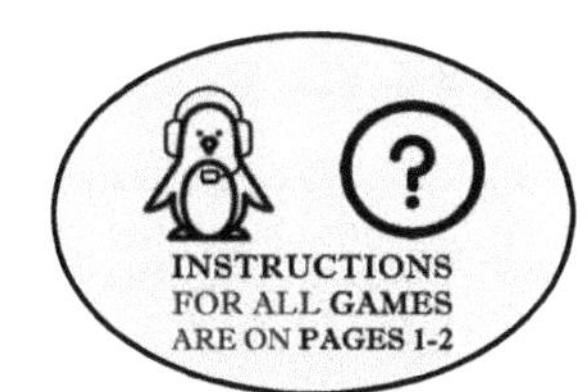

Où vas-tu aller cet été?	*Where are you going to go this summer?*
Comment vas-tu voyager?	*How are you going to travel?*
Combien de temps vas-tu passer là-bas?	*How long are you going to spend over there?*
Où vas-tu rester?	*Where are you going to stay?*
Qu'est-ce que tu vas faire pendant les vacances?	*What are you going to do during the holidays?*

Cet été, je vais aller en vacances en *This summer I am going to go on holiday to* **Nous allons aller en** *We are going to go to*	Allemagne Angleterre Bourgogne Bretagne Espagne	**en avion** *by plane* **en bateau** *by boat* **en car** *by coach* **en voiture** *by car*	
Je vais passer… *I am going to spend* **Nous allons passer…** *We are going to spend*	**une semaine** *1 week* **deux semaines** *2 weeks*	**là-bas** *over there* **avec ma famille** *with my family*	**Ce sera ennuyeux** *It will be boring*
Je vais rester dans *I am going to stay in* **Nous allons rester dans** *We are going to stay in*	**la maison de ma famille** **un camping** **un hôtel bon marché** *a cheap hotel* **un hôtel de luxe** *a luxury hotel*		**Ce sera amusant** *It will be fun*
Je vais… *I am going to…* **Nous allons…** *We are going to…* **J'aimerais…** **Je voudrais…** *I would like to…* **Nous aimerions…** **Nous voudrions…** *We would like to…*	**acheter des souvenirs** *buy souvenirs* **aller à la plage** *go to the beach* **aller en boîte** *go clubbing* **bronzer** *sunbathe* **danser** *dance* **faire des courses** *go shopping* **faire de la plongée** *go scuba diving* **faire du sport** *do sport* **faire du tourisme** *go sightseeing* **faire du vélo** *go biking* **jouer avec des amis** *play with some friends* **jouer de la guitare** *play the guitar* **manger et dormir** *eat and sleep* **manger de la nourriture délicieuse** *eat delicious food* **me/nous reposer** *rest* **sortir en ville** *go out into town*		**Ce sera génial** *It will be great*

UNIT 15 – FIND SOMEONE WHO – Student Cards

Cet été, je vais aller en vacances en Angleterre avec ma famille. Nous allons voyager en bateau. Nous allons passer une semaine là-bas. **IRÈNE**	Cet été, je vais aller en vacances en Chine avec ma famille. Nous allons y aller en car. Nous allons passer deux semaines là-bas. **JULIETTE**	Cet été, je vais aller en vacances en Écosse avec ma famille. Nous allons voyager en bateau. Nous allons passer cinq jours là-bas. **HUGO**	Cet été, je vais aller en vacances à Cannes avec mon amie Martine. Nous allons y aller en avion. Nous allons passer une semaine et demie là-bas. **CAROLINE**
Cet été, je vais aller en vacances en Italie avec ma famille. Nous allons y aller en car. Nous allons passer quatre semaines là-bas. **CLAIRE**	Cet été, je vais aller en vacances en Chine avec ma famille. Nous allons y aller en avion. Nous allons passer trois semaines là-bas. **LÉA**	Cet été, je vais aller en vacances au Japon avec mon oncle et ma tante. Nous allons voyager en bateau. Nous allons passer trois semaines là-bas. **BRUNO**	Cet été, je vais aller en vacances en Corée avec mon petit ami. Nous allons y aller en avion. Nous allons passer deux semaines là-bas. **CLAUDIA**
Cet été, je vais aller en vacances aux États-Unis avec mon petit ami. Nous allons voyager en bateau. Nous allons passer huit jours là-bas. **ALICE**	Cet été, je vais aller en vacances au Portugal avec mon frère aîné. Nous allons y aller en voiture. Nous allons passer dix jours là-bas. **THOMAS**	Cet été, je vais aller en vacances en Allemagne avec mes amis. Nous allons y aller en train. Nous allons passer une semaine là-bas. **ADRIEN**	Cet été, je vais aller en vacances en Martinique avec ma petite amie. Nous allons voyager en bateau. Nous allons passer dix jours là-bas. **JULIEN**
Cet été, je vais aller en vacances au Maroc avec ma famille. Nous allons voyager en bateau. Nous allons passer six jours là-bas. **HÉLÈNE**	Cet été, je vais aller en vacances au Japon avec ma petite amie. Nous allons voyager en bateau. Nous allons passer un mois là-bas. **LAURENT**	Cet été, je vais aller en vacances en Écosse avec mes trois frères. Nous allons y aller en voiture. Nous allons passer quinze jours là-bas. **GAËL**	Cet été, je vais aller en vacances en Irlande avec mes deux frères. Nous allons voyager en bateau. Nous allons passer trois semaines là-bas. **SERGE**

Find someone who...		**Name**
1.	...is going to go by boat to England.	
2.	...is going to spend their holiday in Japan.	
3.	...is going on holiday for six days.	
4.	...is going to travel to Malta.	
5.	...is going to go to Japan by boat.	
6.	...is going to go to Portugal.	
7.	...is going to travel by coach.	
8.	...is going to travel by plane to an Asian country.	
9.	...is going to travel with their two brothers.	
10.	...is going on holiday for a month.	
11.	...is going to travel to Germany.	
12.	...is going to spend two weeks in an Asian country.	
13.	...is going to travel by plane to Cuba.	
14.	...is going to go by boat to the USA.	
15.	...is going to travel to Scotland.	

UNIT 15 – FIND SOMEONE WHO – Student Grid
UNIT 15 – ORAL PING PONG – Person A

ENGLISH 1	FRENCH 1	ENGLISH 2	FRENCH 2
This summer I am going to go on holiday to Cannes.	Cet été, je vais aller en vacances à Cannes.	We are going to stay in a cheap hotel.	Nous allons rester dans un hôtel bon marché.
I am going to go to Spain by car.		We are going to rest. It will be relaxing.	
We are going to go to Madagascar by plane.	Nous allons aller à Madagascar en avion.	This summer I am going to go on holiday to Italy.	Cet été, je vais aller en vacances en Italie.
I am going to go to Greece by boat.		We are going to go to Japan by plane.	
We are going to stay in a cheap hotel.	Nous allons rester dans un hôtel bon marché.	I am going to go sightseeing, eat and sleep. It will be relaxing.	Je vais faire du tourisme, manger et dormir. Ce sera relaxant.
We are going to stay in a luxury hotel.		This summer I am going to go on holiday to France. It will be cool.	
I am going to stay on a campsite.	Je vais rester dans un camping.	We are going to buy souvenirs and clothes. It will be fun.	Nous allons acheter des souvenirs et des vêtements. Ce sera amusant.
I am going to go sightseeing. It will be boring.		I am going to play with my friends on the beach.	
I am going to go clubbing. It will be great.	Je vais aller en boîte. Ce sera génial.	We are going to go to the beach. It will be cool.	Je vais aller à la plage. Ce sera cool.
I am going to go out. It will be cool.		I am going to go diving. It will be fun.	

UNIT 15 – ORAL PING PONG – Person B

ENGLISH 1	FRENCH 1	ENGLISH 2	FRENCH 2
This summer I am going to go on holiday to Cuba.		We are going to stay in a cheap hotel.	
I am going to go to Spain by car.	Je vais aller en Espagne en voiture.	We are going to rest. It will be relaxing.	Nous allons nous reposer. Ce sera relaxant.
We are going to go to Mexico by plane.		This summer I am going to go on holiday to Italy.	
I am going to go to Greece by boat.	Je vais aller en Grèce en bateau.	We are going to go to Japan by plane.	Je vais aller au Japon en avion.
We are going to stay in a cheap hotel.		I am going to go sightseeing, eat and sleep. It will be relaxing.	
We are going to stay in a luxury hotel.	Nous allons rester dans un hôtel de luxe.	This summer I am going to go on holiday to France. It will be great.	Cet été, je vais aller en France. Ce sera génial.
I am going to stay on a campsite.		We are going to buy souvenirs and clothes. It will be fun.	
I am going to go sightseeing. It will be boring.	Je vais faire du tourisme. Ce sera ennuyeux.	I am going to play with my friends on the beach.	Je vais jouer avec mes amis à la plage.
I am going to go clubbing. It will be fun.		We are going to go to the beach. It will be cool.	
I am going to go out. It will be cool.	Je vais sortir. Ce sera cool.	I am going to go diving. It will be interesting.	Je vais faire de la plongée. Ce sera intéressant.

No Snakes No Ladders

7 We are going to rest and sunbathe on the beach.	**8** We are going to go diving and sunbathe.	**23** I am going to go diving. It will be great!	**24** Where are you going to go on holiday?			
6 I am going to go sightseeing and shopping.	**9** We are going to do sport and to go clubbing.	**22** I am going to stay in the family home.	**25** I am going to go clubbing. It will be fun.			
5 What are you going to do?	**10** Where are you going to stay?	**21** I am going to stay on a campsite.	**26** I am going to play with my friends. It will be fun.			
4 I am going to go on holiday to the USA.	**11** I am going to stay in a cheap hotel.	**20** I am going to go to Greece.	**27** What are you going to do?			
3 I am going to go on holiday to France.	**12** We are going to stay in a luxury hotel.	**19** What are you going to do on holiday?	**28** I am going to rest and sunbathe. It wil be relaxing.			
2 I am going to go on holiday to Spain.	**13** How long are you going to spend there?	**18** I am going to go clubbing and dance.	**29** I am going to go out into town every day. It will be interesting.			
1 Where are you going to go on holiday?	**14** I am going to spend a week there.	**17** I am going to eat delicious food.	**30** I am going to do sport, go sightseeing and eat delicious food.			
START	**15** I am going to spend two weeks there.	**16** I am going to spend a month there.	FINISH			

 # No Snakes No Ladders 

DÉPART	1 Où vas-tu aller en vacances?	2 Je vais aller en vacances en Espagne.	3 Je vais aller en vacances en France.	4 Je vais aller en vacances aux États-Unis.	5 Qu'est-ce que tu vas faire?	6 Je vais faire du tourisme et des courses.	7 Nous allons nous reposer et bronzer à la plage.
15 Je vais passer deux semaines là-bas.	14 Je vais passer une semaine là-bas.	13 Combien de temps vas-tu passer là-bas?	12 Nous allons rester dans un hôtel de luxe.	11 Je vais rester dans un hôtel bon marché.	10 Où vas-tu rester?	9 Nous allons faire du sport et aller en boîte.	8 Nous allons faire de la plongée et bronzer.
16 Je vais passer un mois là-bas.	17 Je vais manger de la nourriture délicieuse.	18 Je vais aller en boîte et danser.	19 Qu'est-ce que tu vas faire pendant les vacances?	20 Je vais aller en Grèce.	21 Je vais rester dans un camping.	22 Je vais rester dans la maison de ma famille.	23 Je vais faire de la plongée. Ce sera génial!
ARRIVÉE	30 Je vais faire du sport, faire du tourisme et manger de la nourriture délicieuse.	29 Je vais sortir en ville tous les jours. Ce sera intéressant.	28 Je vais me reposer et bronzer. Ce sera relaxant.	27 Qu'est-ce que tu vas faire?	26 Je vais jouer avec mes amis. Ce sera amusant.	25 Je vais aller en boîte. Ce sera amusant.	24 Où vas-tu aller en vacances?

UNIT 15 – STAIRCASE TRANSLATION

This summer I am going to go on holiday to Argentière with my family.

This summer I am going to go on holiday to Argentière with my family. We are going to go there by plane.

This summer I am going to go on holiday to Argentière with my family. We are going to go there by plane. We are going to stay there for two weeks.

This summer I am going to go on holiday to Argentière with my family. We are going to go there by plane. We are going to stay there for two weeks. We are going to stay in a chalet.

This summer I am going to go on holiday to Argentière with my family. We are going to go there by plane. We are going to stay there for two weeks. We are going to stay in a chalet. We are going to go sightseeing, to eat delicious food, to do sport and to sunbathe.

* This summer I am going to go on holiday to Argentière with my family. We are going to go there by plane. We are going to stay there for two weeks. We are going to stay in chalet. We are going to go sightseeing, to eat delicious food, to do sport and to sunbathe. It will be relaxing and fun.

* Translate the
last step here:

⏱ UNIT 15 – FASTER! 🚀

Say:

1. Next summer I am going to go on holiday.
2. I am going to go to Spain.
3. I am going to travel by plane.
4. I am going to spend a week there.
5. I am going to stay in a luxury hotel.
6. I am going to go to the beach every day.
7. I am going to sunbathe.
8. I am going to play with my friends.
9. I am going to go diving.
10. It will be relaxing and fun.

	Time	Mistakes	Referee's name
1			
2			
3			
4			

UNIT 15 – FLUENCY CARDS

COUNTRY	TRANSPORT	DURATION	ACCOMMODATION	ACTIVITIES
Spain		One week	★ ★ ★	
Italy		Five days	★ ★ ★ ★	
Greece		Two weeks		
France		One month	*family house*	
Germany		Ten days		

	Time	Mistakes
1.		
2.		
3.		
4.		

UNIT 15 – COMMUNICATIVE DRILLS

1	2	3
Where are you going on holiday? - I am going to go to England. **Who are you going with?** - I am going there with my family. **How long are you going to spend there?** -We are going to spend two weeks there. **Where are you going to stay?** - We are going to stay in a cheap hotel in London. **What are you going to do?** - We are going to go sightseeing, go shopping and go clubbing. It will be cool.	**Where are you going on holiday?** - I am going to go to Spain. **Who are you going with?** - I am going there with my friends. **How long are you going to spend there?** - We are going to spend ten days there. **Where are you going to stay?** - We are going to stay in a luxury hotel near Barcelona. **What are you going to do?** We are going to the beach, sunbathe, play football and go clubbing. It will be fun.	**Where are you going on holiday?** - I am going to go to France. **Who are you going with?** - I am going there with my family. **How long are you going to spend there?** - We are going to spend three weeks there. **Where are you going to stay?** - We are going to stay in a cheap hotel in Paris and a luxury hotel in Nice. **What are you going to do?** - We are going to go sightseeing, buy clothes and souvenirs and eat delicious food. It will be great.
4	5	6
Where are you going on holiday? - I am going to go to Greece. **Who are you going with?** - I am going there with my uncle and my aunt. **How long are you going to spend there?** - We are going to spend ten days. **Where are you going to stay?** - We are going to stay in a cheap hotel in Santorini. **What are you going to do?** - We are going to go diving, horse riding and rest. It will be relaxing.	**Where are you going on holiday?** - I am going to go to Portugal. **Who are you going with?** - I am going there with my grandparents. **How long are you going to spend there?** - We are going to spend two weeks there. **Where are you going to stay?** - We are going to stay in my family's home in Lisbon. **What are you going to do?** - We are going to eat, sleep, watch television and go sightseeing. It will be a bit boring.	**Where are you going on holiday?** - I am going to go to Madagascar. **Who are you going with?** - I am going there with my family. **How long are you going to spend there?** - We are going to spend two weeks there. **Where are you going to stay?** - We are going to stay in a luxury hotel in Sainte-Marie. **What are you going to do?** - We are going to go sightseeing, diving, shopping and clubbing. I am also going to go rock climbing and do cycling. It will be cool and fun.

UNIT 15 – COMMUNICATIVE DRILLS
REFEREE CARD

1	2	3
Où vas-tu aller en vacances? - Je vais aller en Angleterre. **Avec qui vas-tu y aller?** - Je vais y aller avec ma famille. **Combien de temps vas-tu passer là-bas?** - Nous allons passer deux semaines là-bas. **Où vas-tu rester?** - Nous allons rester dans un hôtel bon marché à Londres. **Qu'est-ce que tu vas faire?** - Nous allons faire du tourisme, faire des courses et aller en boîte. Ce sera cool.	**Où vas-tu aller en vacances?** - Je vais aller en Espagne. **Avec qui vas-tu y aller?** - Je vais y aller avec mes amis. **Combien de temps vas-tu passer là-bas?** - Nous allons passer dix jours là-bas. **Où vas-tu rester?** - Nous allons rester dans un hôtel de luxe près de Barcelone. **Qu'est-ce que tu vas faire?** - Nous allons aller à la plage, bronzer, jouer au foot et aller en boîte. Ce sera amusant.	**Où vas-tu aller en vacances?** - Je vais aller en France. **Avec qui vas-tu y aller?** - Je vais y aller avec ma famille. **Combien de temps vas-tu passer là-bas?** - Nous allons passer trois semaines là-bas. **Où vas-tu rester?** - Nous allons rester dans un hôtel bon marché à Paris et dans un hôtel de luxe à Nice. **Qu'est-ce que tu vas faire?** - Nous allons faire du tourisme, acheter des vêtements et des souvenirs et manger de la nourriture délicieuse. Ce sera génial.

4	5	6
Où vas-tu aller en vacances? - Je vais aller en Grèce. **Avec qui vas-tu y aller?** - Je vais y aller avec mon oncle et ma tante. **Combien de temps vas-tu passer là-bas?** - Nous allons passer dix jours là-bas. **Où vas-tu rester?** - Nous allons rester dans un hôtel bon marché à Santorini. **Qu'est-ce que tu vas faire?** - Nous allons faire de la plongée, faire de l'équitation et nous reposer. Ce sera relaxant.	**Où vas-tu aller en vacances?** - Je vais aller au Portugal. **Avec qui vas-tu y aller?** - Je vais y aller avec mes grands-parents. **Combien de temps vas-tu passer là-bas?** - Nous allons passer deux semaines là-bas. **Où vas-tu rester?** - Nous allons rester dans la maison de ma famille à Lisbonne. **Qu'est-ce que tu vas faire?** - Nous allons manger, dormir, regarder la télé et faire du tourisme. Ce sera un peu ennuyeux.	**Où vas-tu aller en vacances?** - Je vais aller à Madagascar. **Avec qui vas-tu y aller?** - Je vais y aller avec ma famille. **Combien de temps vas-tu passer là-bas?** - Nous allons passer deux semaines là-bas. **Où vas-tu rester?** - Nous allons rester dans un hôtel de luxe à Sainte-Marie. **Qu'est-ce que tu vas faire?** - Nous allons faire du tourisme, faire de la plongée, faire des courses et aller en boîte. Je vais aussi faire de l'escalade et du vélo. Ce sera cool et amusant.

UNIT 15 – SURVEY

	What is your name?	Where are you going to go on holidays?	Who are you going on holidays with?	How long are you going to stay there?	Where are you going to stay?	What are you going to do during the holidays?
	Comment tu t'appelles?	Où vas-tu aller en vacances?	Avec qui vas-tu aller en vacances?	Combien de temps vas-tu passer là-bas?	Où vas-tu rester?	Qu'est-ce que tu vas faire pendant les vacances?
e.g.	*Je m'appelle Thomas.*	*Je vais aller en vacances en Corse en bateau.*	*Je vais y aller avec mon ami Denis.*	*Je vais passer deux semaines là-bas.*	*Je vais rester dans la maison de ma famille.*	*Je vais faire du sport, manger et dormir.*
1.						
2.						
3.						
4.						
5.						
6.						
7.						

UNIT 15 – ANSWERS

FIND SOMEONE WHO

	Find someone who...	Name
1.	...is going to go by boat to England.	Irène
2.	...is going to spend their holiday in Japan.	Bruno / Laurent
3.	...is going on holiday for six days.	Hélène
4.	...is going to travel to Martinique	Julien
5.	...is going to go to Japan by boat.	Bruno / Laurent
6.	...is going to go to Portugal.	Thomas
7.	...is going to travel by coach.	Juliette / Claire
8.	...is going to travel by plane to an Asian country.	Léa / Claudia
9.	...is going to travel with their two brothers.	Serge
10.	...is going on holiday for a month.	Laurent
11.	...is going to travel to Germany.	Adrien
12.	...is going to spend two weeks in an Asian country.	Claudia / Juliette
13.	...is going to travel by plane to Cannes.	Caroline
14.	...is going to go by boat to USA.	Alice
15.	...is going to travel to Scotland.	Gaël / Hugo

STAIRCASE TRANSLATION

Cet été, je vais aller en vacances à Argentière avec ma famille. Nous allons y aller en avion. Nous allons passer deux semaines là-bas. Nous allons rester dans un chalet. Nous allons faire du tourisme, manger de la nourriture délicieuse, faire du sport et bronzer. Ce sera relaxant et amusant.

FASTER! REFEREE SOLUTION:

1. L'été prochain, je vais aller en vacances.
2. Je vais aller en Espagne.
3. Je vais voyager en avion.
4. Je vais passer une semaine là-bas.
5. Je vais rester dans un hôtel de luxe.
6. Je vais aller à la plage tous les jours.
7. Je vais bronzer.
8. Je vais jouer avec mes amis.
9. Je vais faire de la plongée.
10. Ce sera relaxant et amusant.

FLUENCY CARDS

1. Cet été, je vais aller en Espagne. Je vais voyager en voiture et je vais passer une semaine là-bas. Je vais rester dans un hôtel trois étoiles. Je vais bronzer et je vais faire de la plongée.
2. Cet été, je vais aller en Italie. Je vais voyager en train et je vais passer cinq jours là-bas. Je vais rester dans un hôtel quatre étoiles. Je vais acheter des souvenirs et faire du vélo.
3. Cet été, je vais aller en Grèce. Je vais voyager en bateau et je vais passer deux semaines là-bas. Je vais rester dans un camping. Je vais aller à la plage et bronzer.
4. Cet été, je vais aller en France. Je vais voyager en avion et je vais passer un mois là-bas. Je vais rester dans la maison de ma famille. Je vais prendre des photos et faire du tourisme/visiter des monuments.
5. Cet été, je vais aller en Allemagne. Je vais voyager en car et je vais passer dix jours là-bas. Je vais rester dans un hôtel bon marché. Je vais faire des courses et me reposer/dormir.